SCHOLASTIC

Vocabulary
Games & Activities
That Boost Reading and Writing Skills

by Immacula A. Rhodes

New York • Toronto • London • Auckland • Sydney
Mexico City • New Delhi • Hong Kong • Buenos Aires

Teaching
Resources

To Alan and Amber,
You give definition to my life.

∙∙

*"Trust in the Lord with all your heart
and lean not on your own understanding;
in all your ways acknowledge him,
and he will make your paths straight."*
—PROVERBS 3: 5-6

Editor: Joan Novelli
Cover and interior design by Holly Grundon
Interior illustrations by Teresa Anderko

ISBN-13: 978-0-439-66545-2
ISBN-10: 0-439-66545-0

1 2 3 4 5 6 7 8 9 10   40   16 15 14 13 12 11 10 09

Contents

Games and Activities

Supplemental Word Charts and Lists

Introduction

Vocabulary Games & Activities That Boost Reading and Writing Skills is a collection of fun, reproducible games and activities designed to support vocabulary instruction by helping students explore and interact with a wide range of words—from what they mean and how they're used to how they are formed and where they come from. These vocabulary-building games and activities actively engage students in sharing their word knowledge, exploring word derivatives, analyzing and building words, developing strategies for recalling and strengthening vocabulary, and demonstrating what they learn—all skills that promote a broader vocabulary and deeper word knowledge.

Skills and concepts featured in this book include affixes, Latin and Greek roots, synonyms, antonyms, multiple meaning words, analogies, heteronyms, homophones, compound words, and more. As students engage in the activities, they build on prior word knowledge, use critical thinking skills, make connections to other words and concepts, and express what they learn in their own words—an important step in demonstrating true understanding of word meanings and developing "ownership" of words. And, since various games and activities also involve writing the words, students have opportunities to strengthen spelling skills in the process.

What the Research Says

The games and activities in this book are designed with current research in mind. Research shows that explicit vocabulary instruction boosts comprehension and plays a significant role in student achievement (Beck, Perfetti & McKeown, 1982; National Reading Panel, 2000). And, as in other areas of learning, active engagement in vocabulary-learning tasks helps students grow in word knowledge (Blachowicz & Fisher, 2000). Various and repeated opportunities to think about and use words leads to a deeper understanding of their meanings and increases the likelihood that students will make those words a permanent part of their vocabulary repertoire (Beck & McKeown, 2002). Talking about words and their meanings, becoming aware of relationships among words, discussing the use of words in context and creating contexts around them, exploring word structures and origins, and using dictionaries and other reference tools are all important components in enhancing students' word consciousness and building their word-learning strategies. In addition, these types of rich and meaningful language experiences help English Language Learners understand the meaning and use of words, apply word-learning strategies, and develop strong English vocabularies (Block & Mangieri, 2006).

How to Use This Book

The materials in *Vocabulary Games & Activities That Boost Reading and Writing Skills* engage students in active ways to reinforce and build vocabulary. After introducing general or content-area vocabulary, word-analysis skills, or word-building concepts, you can choose the games or activities that address that area of study and use them to provide practice that will strengthen and enhance students' vocabulary and word-learning strategies.

The materials are ideal for working with students in pairs or small groups, or for use in learning centers. The game format encourages students to think out loud, share prior word knowledge and experiences, and use and discuss how words work in context. Through exchanging ideas and information, students can better understand word meanings and uses, expand their vocabularies, and become more confident about making sense of new words they encounter, or using new words as they speak and write. While this exchange of knowledge and ideas is encouraged, students can also use many of the activities individually to practice and reinforce what they've learned. You might also send home the games for students to play with families and friends. Here's what you'll find for each activity:

Players: The number of players listed tells how many players each game or activity setup will accommodate. Make multiple copies of the materials as needed to accommodate the number of students playing. For use with learning center setups, the Directions for Play reproducible (see page 6) also identifies the number of players—helpful information for determining the number of students at the center at any one time.

Skill: See at a glance the specific skill area of focus for each game or activity.

Materials: Use this list to gather materials needed to prepare and play the game or activity, including any reproducible pages and supplies, such as markers or dictionaries.

Getting Ready: Use these guidelines to prepare materials and set up the games and activities.

Teaching Tips: The tips in this section offer suggestions for using the games and activities, including information related to preparing materials, introducing concepts, and using the game or activity to enhance or assess learning.

Extension Activities: These suggestions provide additional practice in the targeted skill and provide ways to adapt the activity or materials to further reinforce vocabulary.

Directions for Play: Copy the reproducible Directions for Play for each game and review them with students before they play. Point out the Playing Tips section, which offers helpful information. Laminate the Directions for Play if desired and store the directions with the game. Note that some games and activities invite students to collaborate. This noncompetitive format encourages students to pool their knowledge, voice their thoughts, and share ideas.

Teaching Tip

To help students really think about words and their meanings, games such as Definition Dive (page 11) and Word Wiz (page 15) ask students to give examples and non-examples of a targeted word. For instance, for the word *energetic*, students might offer examples such as *active, very lively, hardworking*, or *on the go*. Non-examples might include *lazy, drowsy*, or *without enthusiasm*. Other games, such as Pharoah's Prefix Pyramid (page 20) or Go Greek! (page 62), ask students to give examples of how a word is used or to use it in a sentence. For the word *thermometer*, for example, a student might respond that a thermometer tells the temperature. Or, the student might use the word in a sentence, such as "When we checked the thermometer this morning, it was already 75 degrees!"

Customizing the Games and Activities

The games and activities in this book can easily be modified to expand their use and provide additional practice and reinforcement. Some games include extra blank game boards and game cards, which you can customize with new vocabulary. For others, simply mask existing words on the appropriate reproducible pages, then make copies and fill in new vocabulary. The charts and lists on pages 138–144 are a good source of additional words, as is vocabulary drawn from classroom lessons and activities.

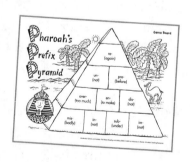

You can also narrow the scope of some activities by selecting only the words or specific skills you want to reinforce. To do this, simply use the game cards and components that you want students to work with, or mask words or sections on the reproducible pages to help students focus only on particular skills or concepts. For example, you can mask blocks on the game board for Pharoah's Prefix Pyramid (page 22) to reduce the number of prefixes students will work with.

Classroom Management Tips

Following are general tips to help make preparation, use, and storage a breeze.

✻ Prepare the games and activities in advance or invite students to help you make them.

✻ For durability, laminate the game boards, game cards, spinners, and other game pieces.

✻ Store each assembled game and game pieces, along with the Directions for Play, in a gallon-sized resealable plastic bag.

✻ Designate an area to store the games, such as in a vertical file tray or file box, on a bookshelf, or in a basket at the reading center or other learning center.

Using the Charts and Lists

On pages 138–144, you'll find charts and lists of prefixes, suffixes, Latin and Greek roots, heteronyms, homophone pairs, and words borrowed from other languages. You can use these pages as reference for your own use—they're a great resource to have on hand whenever you need to check the meaning of an affix or root or want to share examples of words in one of these categories. Here are some additional ways you can use them with students:

✻ Use the lists to adapt or expand the activities and games.

✻ Copy, laminate, and display these pages for reference in reading, writing, or literacy centers. (You might enlarge the pages for this purpose.) Encourage students to browse the charts and lists, as well, to nurture an interest in language.

✻ Invite students to use the lists (or parts of them) in scavenger hunts. They can search print materials for particular heteronyms, homophones, words from other languages, or find words that contain specific affixes or roots. Encourage students to explore how the words they find are used in different contexts.

✻ Send home copies of the pages to include families in their students' word-learning activities.

✻ To encourage wordplay, invite students to use the lists of affixes and roots (pages 138–141) to create their own words. Have them share their words and meanings and demonstrate how each word might be used. Then ask them to name actual words that have similar word parts, meanings, and uses. Encourage students to compare the made-up and actual words.

12 Terrific Tips

Here are useful tips to follow before, during, and after using the games and activities.

 1 Review the materials and directions, and demonstrate how to use each game or activity. Provide suggestions on how to determine the order in which players take turns, such as rolling a number cube and taking turns in numerical order.

 2 As students participate in games and activities, encourage interaction and discussion. These active exchanges of information and knowledge enrich students' understanding of the meanings and uses of words, and reinforce and clarify word concepts.

 3 Use the games and activities to build vocabulary with the words provided, as well as with words you (or your students) choose for general vocabulary study or from literature or content areas. (See Customizing the Games and Activities, page 6.)

 4 Engage in the activities with students. This can be a fun way to interview and observe students, and informally assess their word knowledge. Conduct mini-lessons to review the words, skills, or concepts used in each activity or game as needed.

 5 Encourage students to use the actual words being learned. The more they say and hear a word, the more likely they will incorporate it into their own vocabulary.

 6 Keep a dictionary and thesaurus on hand. Knowing how to use word reference tools is a skill students need to develop. Guide students in integrating what they discover in these references with their own knowledge of words, information they've gathered from others, and context clues.

7 Provide students with sticky notes to use during activities and games. Encourage students to jot down words they want to explore further, or questions that come up about particular words, concepts, or strategies. Follow up with a Word Talk to share and discuss their discoveries, questions, and connections. (Students can also flag unfamiliar or intriguing words in the print materials they read to discuss and explore with the class later.)

8 Create a word-rich environment with word walls, quote displays, and word games and puzzles. Reinforce and share students' excitement about discovering new words and their meanings.

9 Have students journal about interesting words or phrases they encounter. Ask them to include why the words stuck and how they might use them in their own conversations and writing activities. Encourage students to add to their journal entries as they learn more about words already included in them.

10 Post prompts in the writing center to encourage students to use the words they learn. You can use their writing as part of an assessment.

11 Look for opportunities to use words (and concepts) featured in the games and activities in class conversations. When students come across an unfamiliar word, take time to discuss the word and point out strategies that help them explore its meaning and use. For some words, you might refer students to a particular game board, answer key, chart, or word list in this book to help them explore and learn more.

12 Use the words, skills, and word-building concepts and strategies that are built into the games and activities to teach and reinforce related spelling and grammar rules. Students can use many of the game cards as flash cards, or make their own based on words they construct in the activities. You might place the cards in the writing or spelling center to reinforce particular vocabulary and related skills.

Connections to the Standards

This book is designed to support you in meeting the following reading and writing standards outlined by Mid-continent Research for Education and Learning (McREL), an organization that collects and synthesizes national and state standards.

Uses the general skills and strategies of the reading process.

- Uses phonetic and structural analysis techniques, syntactic structure, and semantic context to decode unknown words
- Understands level-appropriate sight words and vocabulary, including synonyms, antonyms, homophones, and multi-meaning words
- Uses context clues, definition, restatement, example, and comparison and contrast to verify word meanings
- Uses knowledge of analogies to infer the meaning of phrases
- Knows denotative and connotative meanings of words
- Knows vocabulary related to different content areas and current events
- Uses word reference materials, including dictionary and thesaurus
- Uses Latin and Greek roots, affixes, and meanings of frequently used foreign words to understand word meaning

Uses grammatical and mechanical conventions in written compositions.

- Writes in complete sentences
- Uses pronouns, nouns, verbs, adjectives, and adverbs in writing
- Spells high frequency and commonly misspelled words
- Uses compounds, roots, suffixes, prefixes, and syllable constructions in spelling
- Uses a dictionary and other resources to spell words

Source: Kendall, J. S. & Marzano, R. J. (2004). *Content knowledge: A compendium of standards and benchmarks for K–12 education.* Aurora, CO: Mid-continent Research for Education and Learning. Online database: http://www.mcrel.org/standards-benchmarks/.

Resources and References

Beck, I. L., McKeown, M. G., & Kucan, L. (2002). *Bringing words to life: Robust vocabulary instruction.* New York: Guilford Press.

Beck, I. L., Perfetti, C. A., & McKeown, M. G. (1982). The effects of long-term vocabulary instruction on lexical access and reading comprehension. *Journal of Educational Psychology,* 74(4), 506–21.

Blachowicz, C. L. Z. & Fisher, P. (2000). Vocabulary instruction. In M. L. Kamil, P. Mosenthal, P. D. Pearson, & R. Barr (Eds.), *Handbook of reading research* (Vol. 3, pp. 503–523). Mahwah, NJ: Erlbaum.

Block, C. C. & Mangieri, J. N. (2006). *The vocabulary-enriched classroom: Practices for improving the reading performance of all students in grades 3 and up.* New York: Scholastic.

Kendall, J. S. & Marzano, R. J. (2004). *Content knowledge: A compendium of standards and benchmarks for K–12 education.* Aurora, CO: Mid-continent Research for Education and Learning. Online database: http://www.mcrel.org/standards-benchmarks/.

McLaughlin, M. & Fisher, L. (2005). *Research-based reading lessons for K–3.* New York: Scholastic.

National Reading Panel. (2000). *Teaching children to read: An evidence-based assessment of the scientific research literature on reading and its implications for reading instruction: Report of the subgroups.* (NIH Publication No. 00–4754). Washington, DC: National Institute of Child Health and Human Development.

Definition Dive

Children dive into words to develop deeper understanding of their meanings.

Players: Any number

Skill: General or content area vocabulary

Getting Ready

Copy the Directions for Play and word cards. Color the word cards. Laminate all game components, then cut apart the word cards. Use the wipe-off pen to write a vocabulary word of your choice on each card. (Prepare as many cards as the number of words you want students to work with.) Copy a supply of record sheets for players.

Teaching Tips

⊙ Use this activity with pairs, small groups, or the whole class to teach and review general or content area vocabulary. Have all students complete the record sheet for the same word and then review and discuss their responses together. You might also use the activity with individuals to introduce and reinforce specific words a student needs to know.

⊙ Read the selected word card with students. Read the word, pronounce it several times to reinforce how it sounds, and have students say the word. Point out spelling patterns or characteristics that help students remember the word's pronunciation or spelling. Invite students to share what they know about the meaning and use of the word.

Materials

⊙ Directions for Play (page 12)

⊙ Definition Dive word cards and record sheet (pages 13–14)

⊙ wipe-off pen

⊙ pencils and crayons

Extension Activity

Have students alphabetize and place their completed record sheets in three-ring binders, adding more sheets as they complete them. You might have students use the record sheets to make separate booklets for words related to a specific content area. Students can use their binders or booklets as a word reference tool for reading or writing activities.

Definition Dive

1 Choose a word card.

2 Say the word. Think about what you know about the meaning and use of the word.

3 Write the word in the boat on the record sheet.

4 Follow the directions at the first level. After you complete this level, "dive" deeper by coloring the arrow on the right and moving to the next level.

5 Continue diving deeper and completing each section until you reach the treasure at the bottom of the sea.

Players:
Any number

Materials

- ◎ word cards
- ◎ record sheets
- ◎ pencils and crayons

- ◎ Share what you know about the word with other players.

- ◎ Use a dictionary for help if needed.

Vocabulary Games & Activities That Boost Reading and Writing Skills © 2009 by Immacula A. Rhodes. Scholastic Teaching Resources

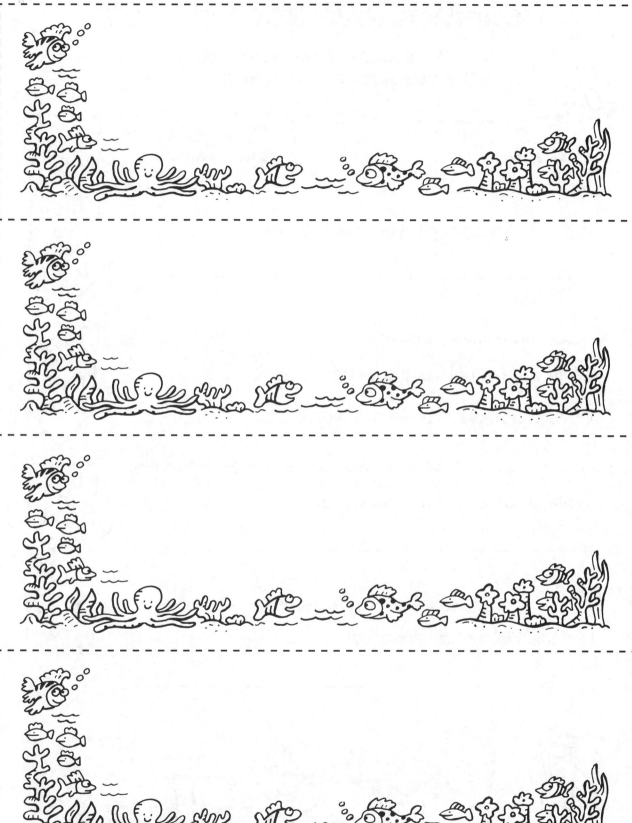

Definition Dive Record Sheet

Write a vocabulary word on the boat.
Complete each level. Then color the diver.

Word: _____

Write the meaning in your own words:

_____

Dive to next level.

Write an example of the word: _____

Write a non-example of the word: _____

Dive to next level.

Write a sentence with the word:

_____

Dive to next level.

Use the word in another way:

_____

Dive to next level.

Word Wiz

Students share prior knowledge and ideas to explore vocabulary words.

Players: 3–4

Skill: General and content area vocabulary

Getting Ready

Copy the Directions for Play, game board, and word cards. Color the game board and word cards. Laminate all game components, then cut apart the cards. Use a wipe-off pen to write a vocabulary word on each card. (Use as many cards as the number of words you want students to work with; each player will need a card.) Copy a supply of record sheets for players.

Teaching Tip

When preparing word cards for the activity, use general or content area vocabulary words. Or use homophone pairs, words with common roots, easily confused words, or other types of words that students need extra reinforcement with.

Materials

- Directions for Play (page 16)
- Word Wiz game board, word cards, and record sheet (pages 17–19)
- wipe-off pen
- sticky-note flags (a different color for each player)
- pencils

Extension Activity

Students can cut apart their record sheets by words, alphabetize them, and use an alligator clip or O-ring to bind them together. Students can add to their collection of words as they repeat the game, and use their record sheets as a reference tool for reading or writing activities.

Word Wiz

1 Each player chooses a set of sticky-note flags and places one flag on "Explain." Shuffle the cards and stack them facedown. Each player takes a card from the stack and uses this card for the entire game.

2 Players take turns moving their flag marker to the first space. On your turn, follow the directions using the word on your card.

3 Continue taking turns. Each player moves his or her marker one space at a time around the game board.

- If the space repeats a direction, you must give a different response. For instance, each time you land on "use it in a sentence" you must come up with a new sentence.

- If you have trouble coming up with a response, you may ask other players for help.

4 When you reach *Expert!*, stick the flag marker to the word card. Then set the word card aside.

5 Players choose a new word and play again. Complete a Word Wiz record sheet for each word.

Players: 3–4

Materials

- game board
- word cards
- record sheet
- sticky-note flags
- pencils

After following the directions on a space, players may invite others to add to and discuss their response.

Vocabulary Games & Activities That Boost Reading and Writing Skills © 2009 by Immacula A. Rhodes. Scholastic Teaching Resources

Game Board

Tell more.

Tell its meaning.

Example

Explain

Word Wiz

Give an example.

Give an example.

Use it in a sentence.

Use it in a sentence.

Expert!

Use it in a sentence.

Give a non-example.

It is not like. . .

Extend

It is like. . .

Explore

Word Wiz Word Cards

Word Wiz Record Sheet

Word: _____

Explain
Write the meaning.

_____

_____

Example
Write some examples and non-examples.

_____

_____

_____

Explore

_____ is like
(word)

_____.

_____ is not like
(word)

_____.

Extend
Use the word in sentences.

1. _____

2. _____

3. _____

Congratulations!

Word Wiz Expert

Pharoah's Prefix Pyramid

**Students build a pyramid by combining prefixes
and root words to make new words.**

Players: 2

Skill: Adding prefixes to root words

Getting Ready
Copy the Directions for Play, two game boards, one of each set of game
cards (there are two sets; use a different color paper for each), and the
answer key. Color the game boards. Laminate all game components, then
cut apart the cards.

Teaching Tip
After the game—but while the cards are still in place on the game board—
ask students to write a sentence with each word on their pyramid. Review
the sentences with students to check their understanding.

Materials

- ☉ Directions for Play
  (page 21)
- ☉ Pharoah's Prefix
  Pyramid game board,
  game cards, and
  answer key
  (pages 22–26)
- ☉ dictionary

Extension Activities

- ☉ Place a game board and the game cards in a
  center. Invite student pairs to work together
  to make as many new words as possible by
  combining the prefixes with the root words
  on the cards. Have them list their words on
  a sheet of paper. Later, have all the pairs
  compare the words on their lists. Discuss
  how the prefix in each new word affects the
  meaning of the root word.

- ☉ To provide additional practice, mask the text
  on the game board and fill in a new set of
  prefixes. (See list of prefixes on page 138.)
  Create a new set of game cards to match.

Pharoah's Prefix Pyramid

1 Each player chooses a game board. Select one set of game cards. Shuffle the cards and stack them facedown.

2 To take a turn, select the top card from the stack and read the word. Look at the prefixes on the bottom row of your pyramid. Check to see if you can add one of the prefixes to the word to make a new word.

- If so, say the new word, explain its meaning, and give an example of how it is used. Then place the card on the matching pyramid block.

- Check the answer key. Is your answer correct? If so, take another card.

- Continue your turn until you pick a word that cannot be used to make a new word. Then it is the next player's turn.

- If you cannot make a new word, place the card on the bottom of the stack.

3 Keep taking turns. Players must cover all of the prefix blocks on each row before moving to the next row. The block at the top will be the last block you cover.

4 The first player to "build" a pyramid by covering all of the blocks on his or her game board wins the game.

5 Play again with the second set of cards.

Players: 2

Materials

- ⊙ game board
- ⊙ game cards
- ⊙ answer key
- ⊙ dictionary

- ⊙ If a new word is not on the answer key, players may use a dictionary to check it.

- ⊙ Players may invite others to share what they know about the words they form and give examples of how they are used.

Vocabulary Games & Activities That Boost Reading and Writing Skills © 2009 by Immacula A. Rhodes. Scholastic Teaching Resources

Pharoah's Prefix Pyramid

re-
(again)

un-
(not)

pre-
(before)

over-
(too much)

en-
(to make)

dis-
(not)

mis-
(badly)

in-
(not)

sub-
(under)

im-
(not)

able	achieve	active	agree	basement
behave	connect	courage	cover	direct
eager	equal	game	guide	joy
load	marine	mature	perfect	possible
probable	protect	satisfy	sensitive	sure
trust	usual	view	visible	way

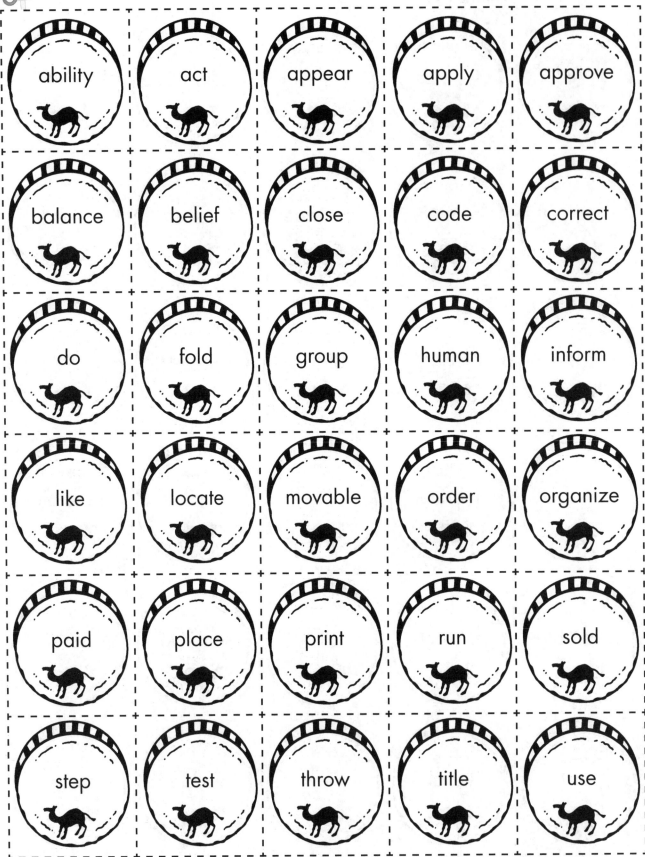

ability	act	appear	apply	approve
balance	belief	close	code	correct
do	fold	group	human	inform
like	locate	movable	order	organize
paid	place	print	run	sold
step	test	throw	title	use

Set 1

Note to Players: These are the most common words made by combining the root words and prefixes in the game. If a word is not shown, check a dictionary to see if the word is correct.

mis-	**in-**	**sub-**	**im-**	**over-**
misbehave	inactive	subbasement	immature	overachieve
misdirect	insensitive	submarine	imperfect	overactive
misguide	invisible	subway	impossible	overeager
mistrust			improbable	overload
				overprotect
				oversensitive
en-	**dis-**	**un-**	**pre-**	**re-**
enable	disable	unable	pregame	reactive
encourage	disagree	uncover	preload	reconnect
enjoy	disconnect	unequal	premature	recover
ensure	discourage	unload	preview	redirect
entrust	discover	unsure		reload
	dissatisfy	unusual		review
	distrust			

Set 2

Note to Players: These are the most common words made by combining the root words and prefixes in the game. If a word is not shown, check a dictionary to see if the word is correct.

mis-	in-	sub-	im-	over-
misapply	inability	subgroup	imbalance	overact
miscode	incorrect	subhuman	immovable	overcorrect
misinform	inhuman	suborder		overdo
misplace		subtest		overpaid
misprint		subtitle		overprint
misstep				overrun
misuse				oversold
				overstep
				overthrow
				overuse

en-	dis-	un-	pre-	re-
enact	disability	unbalance	preapprove	react
enclose	disappear	unbelief	preorder	reappear
encode	disapprove	undo	prepaid	reapply
enfold	disbelief	unfold	preprint	rebalance
entitle	disclose	ungroup	pretest	recode
	dislike	unlike		redo
	dislocate	unmovable		refold
	disorder	unpaid		regroup
	disorganize	unsold		relocate
	displace			reorder
	disuse			reorganize
				repaid
				replace
				reprint
				rerun
				resold
				retest
				reuse

Vocabulary Games & Activities That Boost Reading and Writing Skills © 2009 by Immacula A. Rhodes. Scholastic Teaching Resources

Number Prefix-O!

Students explore the meaning of words that contain number or quantity prefixes.

Players: 2–4, plus a caller

Skill: Identifying number and quantity prefixes

Getting Ready

Copy the Directions for Play, game boards, game cards, and answer key. Laminate all game components, then cut apart the game boards and cards.

Teaching Tips

⊙ Before beginning the game, one child should be named the official "caller." Depending on the needs of the students, the teacher may want to assign this role, or children may volunteer or select a caller from within the group.

⊙ At the end of the game, have players take turns calling out each covered word on their game boards. Invite all players, including the caller, to explain the meaning of each word and give examples of its use. (Keep a dictionary on hand for students to look up meanings of unfamiliar words.)

Materials

⊙ Directions for Play (page 28)

⊙ Number Prefix-O! game boards, game cards, and answer key (pages 29–34)

⊙ game markers (such as plastic counters)

Extension Activity

Prepare and display a large chart that shows the number prefixes and their meanings. Have students refer to the chart as they brainstorm a list of words that contain number prefixes. Later, post the chart and list in your writing center. Encourage children to use words from the list in their writing activities.

Number Prefix-O!

1 Before beginning the game, one child should be named the official "caller."

2 Each player chooses a game board and 16 game markers. The caller takes the bag of cards and answer key.

3 The caller draws a card from the bag and reads the number aloud.

4 Check the words on your game board to see if any contain a prefix that represents that number or amount.

- If so, read the word aloud and show it to the caller. The caller checks the answer key to see if the word is a match.

- If correct, cover that space with a marker.

5 Continue playing until one player correctly covers four words in a row (horizontally, vertically, or diagonally) and calls out "Prefix-O!"

Players: 2–4, plus a caller

Materials

- game boards
- game cards
- answer key
- game markers

Players may cover only one space on each turn.

Number Prefix-O!

quarter	decimal	unicorn	octagon
semiannual	duet	triple	century
unite	millimeter	multiplication	bicycle
centennial	quadrant	quintuple	multistory

Number Prefix-O!

centipede	multicolor	duel	tricycle
binoculars	unicycle	quartet	decimeter
quintet	triceratops	octopus	semicircle
multiple	millennium	decade	biweekly

Number Prefix-O!

duplex	decathlon	pentagon	trilogy
multitude	million	octopus	quadrangle
unite	millimeter	decade	semicircle
triangle	century	multicolor	unicorn

Number Prefix-O!

millionaire	octagon	quintet	quadrant
decade	trio	semicolon	unit
bicycle	duplicate	centennial	millimeter
centipede	decimal	pentagram	multigrain

Number Prefix-O! Game Cards

Number Prefix-O!	Number Prefix-O!	Number Prefix-O!	Number Prefix-O!
one	one	two	two
three	three	four	four
five	five	eight	ten
ten	hundred	hundred	thousand
thousand	half	many	many

one (uni)
unicorn
unicycle
unit
unite

two (bi, du)
bicycle
binoculars
biweekly
duel
duet
duplex
duplicate

three (tri)
triangle
triceratops
tricycle
trilogy
trio
triple

four (quad, quart)
quadrangle
quadrant
quarter
quartet

five (penta, quint)
pentagon
pentagram
quintet
quintuple

eight (oct)
octagon
octopus

ten (dec)
decade
decathlon
decimal
decimeter

hundred (cent)
centennial
centipede
century

thousand (mille, milli, mill)
millennium
millimeter
million
millionaire

half (semi)
semiannual
semicircle
semicolon

many (multi)
multicolor
multigrain
multiple
multiplication
multistory
multitude

Vocabulary Games & Activities That Boost Reading and Writing Skills © 2009 by Immacula A. Rhodes. Scholastic Teaching Resources

Spin a Suffix

Students "try on" suffixes with different words to create new words.

Players: 2–4

Skill: Adding suffixes to root words

Getting Ready

Copy the Directions for Play, Spin a Suffix Wheel, game cards, and answer key. Color the wheel and glue it to tagboard. Laminate all game components, then cut apart the cards. Use a craft knife to cut the slits in the center of the wheel. Insert the pencil (or straw) through the center until it extends three inches from the bottom. Tape or glue the wheel in place. (Players will spin the wheel like a top.) Copy a supply of record sheets for players.

Teaching Tips

After the game, have students choose one word under each suffix on their record sheets. Ask them to write one or more examples of the word and its use. Then invite students to share and discuss their examples with the other players. Have dictionaries on hand for students to check the meaning and use of their words.

Materials

- Directions for Play (page 36)
- Spin a Suffix Wheel, game cards, record sheet, and answer key (pages 37–40)
- craft knife (teacher use only)
- unsharpened pencil (or sturdy drinking straw)
- packaging tape or craft glue
- pencils

Extension Activity

Use the wheel pattern (page 37) as a template to make additional spinners. Program the new spinners with suffixes you want students to work with. (See page 139 for additional suffixes.) To play, have students spin the spinner, identify the suffix it lands on, and name a word that uses that suffix. Students write the word, explain its meaning, and give examples to demonstrate how the word is used.

Spin a Suffix

1 Each player takes a record sheet and pencil. Shuffle the cards and stack them facedown.

2 To take a turn, spin the wheel (like a top) and read the suffix at the bottom of the wheel.

3 Take the top card from the stack and read the word. Add the suffix to the end of the word. Can you make a new word with the suffix? Check the answer key to see if you are correct.

- If you can make a word, say the word and explain its meaning. Write the word on your record sheet in the column for that suffix. (You may check the word's meaning in a dictionary.) Give examples of how the word is used. Then place the card at the bottom of the stack.

- If you cannot make a new word, place the card on the bottom of the stack.

4 Continue taking turns. The first player to fill in all the lines on his or her record sheet wins the game. (Or continue until all players have filled in their record sheets.)

Players: 2–4

Materials

- ◉ wheel
- ◉ game cards
- ◉ record sheet
- ◉ answer key
- ◉ pencils

- ◉ Players may look up their new word in a dictionary to check its meaning.

- ◉ Players may invite other players to share what they know about the new word.

- ◉ Players may not use a word with the same suffix more than once.

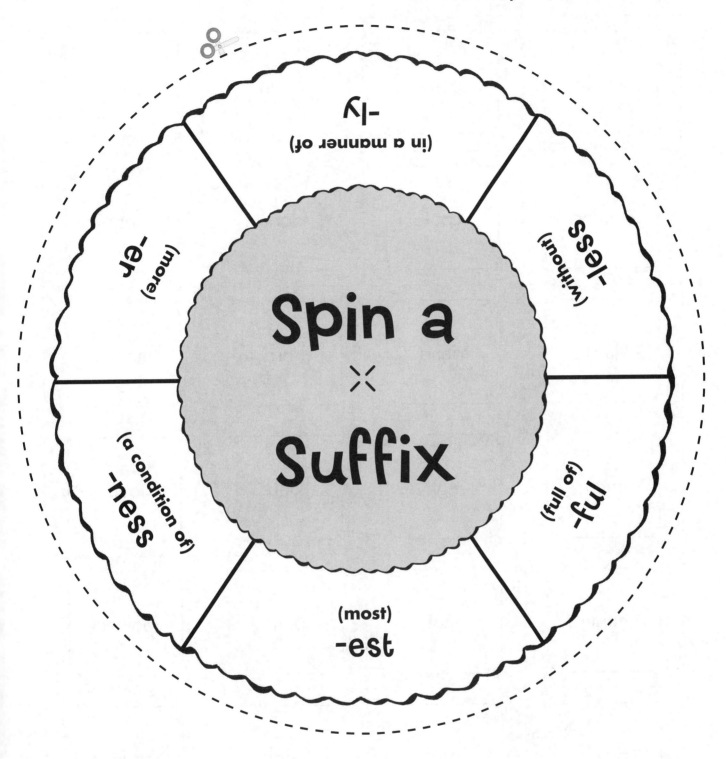

bright	care	clean	color
comfort	cool	dark	fear
firm	friend	hard	harm
help	high	kind	loud
mean	neat	pain	power
quick	short	thank	thought

Spin a Suffix Record Sheet

Add the suffix to the word to see if a word can be made. If so, say the word and its meaning. Check the meaning in a dictionary. If correct, write the word on a line under the suffix.

-er	-est	-ful
1. _____	1. _____	1. _____
2. _____	2. _____	2. _____
3. _____	3. _____	3. _____
4. _____	4. _____	4. _____

-less	-ly	-ness
1. _____	1. _____	1. _____
2. _____	2. _____	2. _____
3. _____	3. _____	3. _____
4. _____	4. _____	4. _____

-er
brighter
cleaner
comforter
cooler
darker
firmer
harder
helper
higher
kinder
louder
meaner
neater
quicker
shorter

-est
brightest
cleanest
coolest
darkest
firmest
hardest
highest
kindest
loudest
meanest
neatest
quickest
shortest

-ful
careful
colorful
fearful
harmful
helpful
painful
powerful
thankful
thoughtful

-less
careless
colorless
comfortless
fearless
friendless
harmless
helpless
kindless
painless
powerless
thankless
thoughtless

-ly
brightly
cleanly
coolly
darkly
firmly
friendly
hardly
highly
kindly
loudly
meanly
neatly
quickly
shortly

-ness
brightness
cleanness
coolness
darkness
firmness
hardness
highness
kindness
loudness
meanness
neatness
quickness
shortness

Suffix Surfer

**Students add suffixes to create
new words and then explore
the meanings of the words.**

Players: 2–4

Skill: Adding suffixes to root words

Getting Ready

Copy the Directions for Play, Suffix Surfer Spinner,
arrow, game cards, and answer key. Color the spinner
pieces. Laminate all game components, then cut apart
the spinner, arrow, and cards. Use the paper fastener
to attach the arrow to the spinner. Copy a supply of
record sheets for players.

Teaching Tips

Before playing the game, review each suffix (and its
variations, if applicable), the meaning, and how its
use changes the meaning—and sometimes spelling—
of root words. Provide several examples of words
containing each suffix. Encourage students to also
give examples and discuss how the suffix affects the
root word in each example.

Materials

- Directions for Play
  (page 42)
- Suffix Surfer Spinner,
  arrow, game cards,
  record sheet, and
  answer key (pages
  43–47)
- paper fastener
- dictionary
- pencils

Extension Activity

Fill in a copy of the record sheet with words
that contain the suffix endings used in the
game. (Refer to the spinner.) For example, you
might use *extension, operation, convertible,
appreciation, submission, productive,
reservation, understandable, donating,* and
reversible. Make a copy for each pair of
students. Then have partners work together to
divide each word into its root word and suffix.
Encourage students to use a dictionary as they
work, and to explain and discuss the meaning
of each word part.

Directions for Play

Suffix Surfer

1 Each player takes a record sheet and pencil. Shuffle the cards and place the stack facedown.

2 To take a turn, spin the spinner and follow the directions. If the spinner lands on a suffix, take the top card and read the word. Add the suffix to the end of the word (or use one of the variations of that suffix listed).

3 Can you make a new word with the suffix? Check the answer key. Is your answer correct?

- If you can make a word, say the word, explain its meaning, and write the word on a surfboard on your record sheet. Give examples of how the word is used. (You may check the word's meaning in a dictionary.) When you are finished, place the card on the bottom of the stack.

- If you cannot make a word, place the card on the bottom of the stack.

4 Continue taking turns. The first player to fill in all of the surfboards on his or her record sheet wins the game. (Or continue until all players have filled in their record sheets.)

Players: 2–4

Materials

- spinner
- game cards
- record sheet
- answer key
- dictionary
- pencils

- Players may invite others to share what they know about the new word.

- Players may not use the same word and suffix combination more than once.

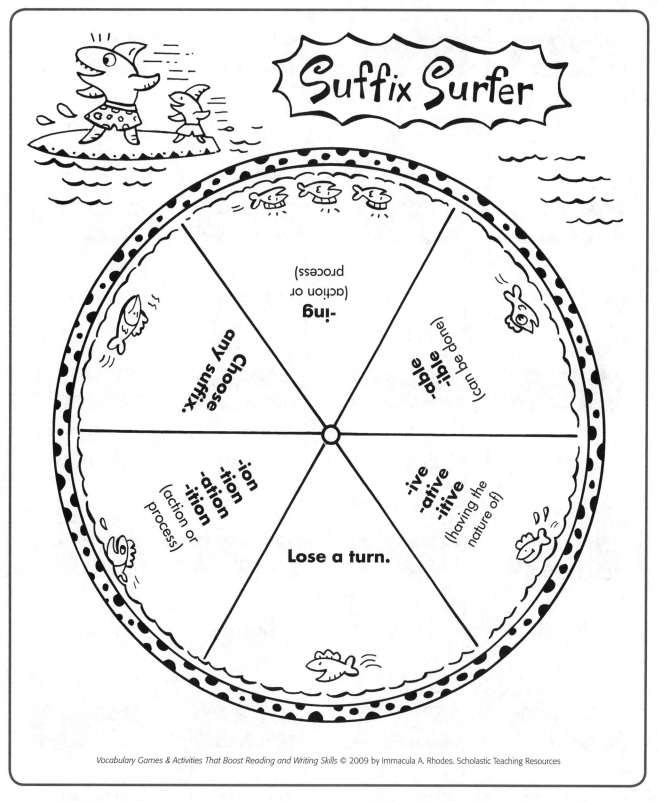

Suffix Surfer

-ing
(action or process)

-able
-ible
(can be done)

-ive
-ative
-itive
(having the nature of)

Lose a turn.

-ion
-tion
-ation
-ition
(action or process)

Choose any suffix.

Paper fastener

Attach arrow to make spinner.

Suffix Surfer Game Cards

Suffix Surfer	Suffix Surfer	Suffix Surfer	Suffix Surfer
accept	act	attract	compare
Suffix Surfer	**Suffix Surfer**	**Suffix Surfer**	**Suffix Surfer**
complete	compute	conserve	construct
Suffix Surfer	**Suffix Surfer**	**Suffix Surfer**	**Suffix Surfer**
control	create	define	destruct
Suffix Surfer	**Suffix Surfer**	**Suffix Surfer**	**Suffix Surfer**
digest	disrupt	educate	exhaust
Suffix Surfer	**Suffix Surfer**	**Suffix Surfer**	**Suffix Surfer**
fascinate	forgive	generate	graduate

Suffix Surfer	Suffix Surfer	Suffix Surfer	Suffix Surfer
imagine	indicate	invent	legislate
manipulate	motivate	narrate	prepare
prevent	product	promote	recognize
reserve	reverse	rotate	sense
suggest	support	transport	vacate

Name: _____ Date: _____

Suffix Surfer Record Sheet

Add the suffix on the spinner to the word.
If it makes a word, write the word on a surfboard.

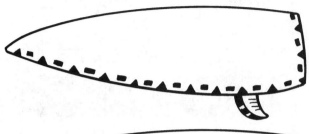

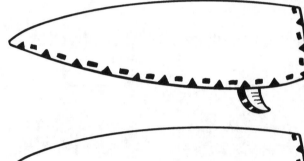

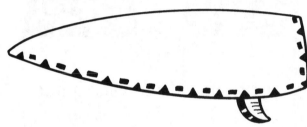

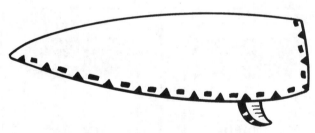
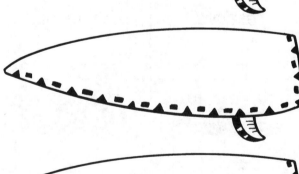

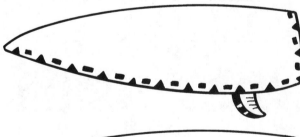

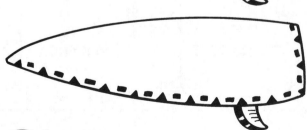

acceptable
accepting

acting
action
active

attracting
attraction
attractive

comparable
comparative
comparing

completing
completion

computable
computation
computing

conservation
conservative
conserving

constructible
constructing
construction

controllable
controlling

creating
creation
creative

definable
defining
definition
definitive

destructible
destructing
destruction
destructive

digestible
digesting
digestion
digestive

disrupting
disruption
disruptive

educable
educating
education
educative

exhaustible
exhausting
exhaustion
exhaustive

fascinating
fascination

forgivable
forgiving

generating
generation
generative

graduating
graduation

imaginable
imaginative
imagination
imagining

indicating
indication
indicative

inventing
invention
inventive

legislating
legislation
legislative

manipulating
manipulation
manipulative

motivating
motivation

narrating
narration
narrative

preparation
preparing

preventable
preventing
prevention
preventive

production
productive

promoting
promotion

recognition
recognizable
recognizing

reservation
reserving

reversing
reversible
reversion

rotating
rotation

sensation
sensible
sensing
sensitive

suggestible
suggesting
suggestion
suggestive

supportable
supporting
supportive

transportable
transportation
transporting

vacating
vacation

Root Suits

**Students create "suits" of words
that have common Latin roots.**

Players: 2–3

Skill: Identifying Latin roots

Getting Ready

Copy the Directions for Play, game boards,
game cards, and answer key. Laminate all game
components, then cut apart the game boards
and game cards on the dashed lines.

Teaching Tips

Before play, review each Latin root featured
in the game, including its meaning. Invite
students to brainstorm words that contain
each root. Write the words on chart paper
and identify the root in each word. Discuss
similarities and differences in the spellings and
meanings of words in each root family. For
additional Latin roots, see page 140.

Materials

- ◉ Directions for Play
  (page 49)

- ◉ Root Suits game
  boards, game cards,
  and answer key
  (pages 50–55)

**Extension
Activities**

- ◉ Place the game boards and game cards at
  a center for individuals or pairs to sort and
  match. Afterward, have students choose a Latin
  root and make a mini-dictionary of words in
  that root family. For each word, have students
  include the meaning, a notation about its
  Latin root, and an example that demonstrates
  its use. If space allows, they might also add
  an illustration. Encourage students to use a
  dictionary as needed.

- ◉ To create new games, mask the words on a
  set of game boards, make copies, then add the
  new roots. Make a new set of word cards to go
  with these roots.

Root Suits

1 Each player takes the same number of game boards and places them faceup on the table.

2 Shuffle the cards and give each player five cards. Stack the remaining cards facedown.

3 To take a turn, check your cards to see if any of your words contain a Latin root shown on any of your game boards. You can think out loud as you work with each root and word.

- Look for spelling parts in the word that are similar to the root.

- Look at the meaning of the root and decide if it helps make sense of the word.

4 Can you make any matches? If so, read the word and place the card in a corner on the matching game board. Then check the answer key. Is each answer correct?

- If so, take a card from the stack to replace that card.

- If not, do one of the following: Take that card back. Or place that card on the bottom of the stack and take a card from the top of the stack to replace it.

5 Continue taking turns. The game ends when one player fills in all the corners on each of his or her game boards, or until players can no longer make matches. The player with the most cards on his or her boards wins the game.

Players: 2–3

Materials

- ⊙ game boards
- ⊙ game cards
- ⊙ answer key

- ⊙ Use only the cards that go with the game boards players are using.

- ⊙ Players may invite others to offer comments about the word and its relationship to the root.

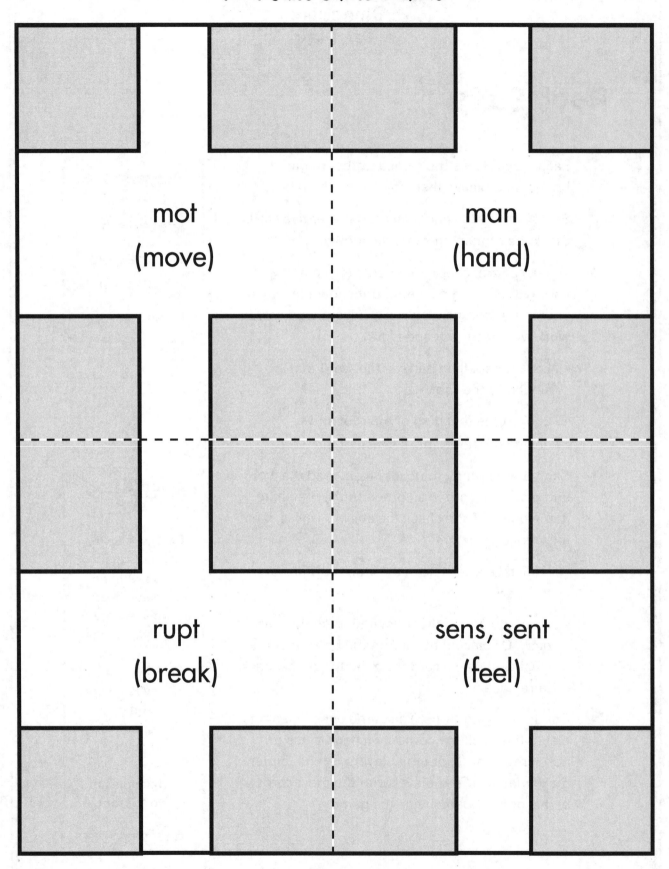

mot
(move)

man
(hand)

rupt
(break)

sens, sent
(feel)

act
(do)

aud
(hear)

fract, frag
(break)

sta
(stand)

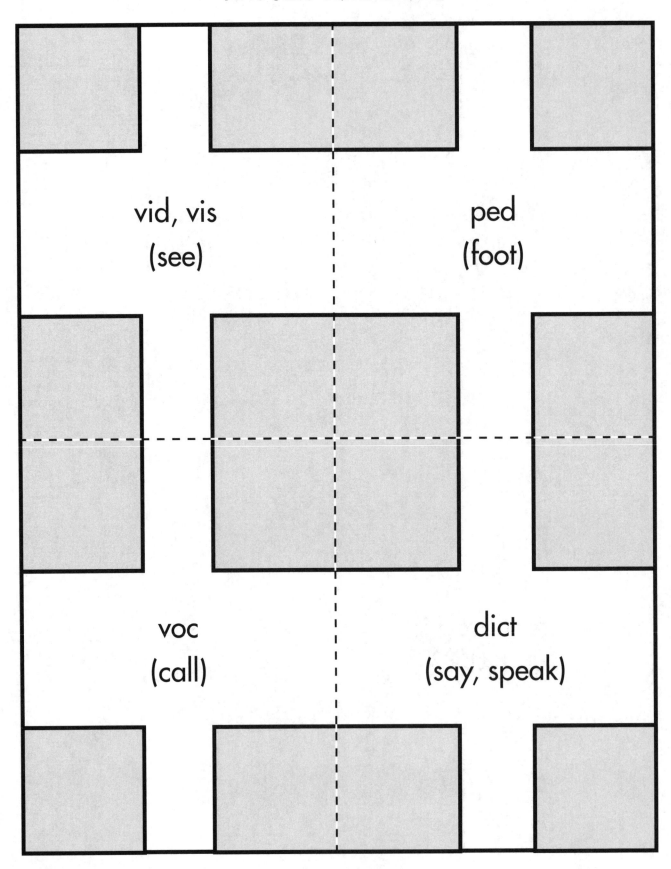

vid, vis
(see)

ped
(foot)

voc
(call)

dict
(say, speak)

Root Suits Game Cards

emotion	motion	motivate	promote
maneuver	manipulate	manual	manuscript
disrupt	erupt	interrupt	rupture
sensation	sensitive	sensory	sentimental
evidence	visible	vision	visual
pedal	pedestal	pedestrian	pedicure

vocabulary	vocal	vocalize	vocation
contradict	dictate	dictionary	predict
action	activate	activity	react
audible	audience	audition	auditory
fraction	fracture	fragile	fragment
stable	station	statue	stature

act
action
activate
activity
react

man
maneuver
manipulate
manual
manuscript

sens, sent
sensation
sentimental
sensitive
sensory

aud
audible
audience
audition
auditory

mot
emotion
motion
motivate
promote

sta
stable
station
statue
stature

dict
contradict
dictate
dictionary
predict

ped
pedal
pedestal
pedestrian
pedicure

vis, vid
evidence
visible
vision
visual

fract, frag
fraction
fracture
fragile
fragment

rupt
disrupt
erupt
interrupt
rupture

voc
vocabulary
vocal
vocalize
vocation

Cube Words

Students make words by combining a variety of Latin prefixes and roots.

Players: 2–4

Skill: Making words with Latin prefixes and roots

Getting Ready

Copy the Directions for Play, number key, number cubes, and answer key. Glue each number cube pattern to tagboard. Laminate all game components, then cut out the number cubes and assemble as shown (page 59). Copy a supply of record sheets for players.

Teaching Tips

Before students do the activity, review the Latin prefixes and roots and their meanings. Write a few examples of words that contain a prefix-root combination from the activity. Underline the prefix and root in each word to demonstrate how the parts come together to form the word. Then discuss each word's meaning and give examples of its use.

Materials

⊙ Directions for Play (page 57)

⊙ Cube Words number key, number cubes, record sheet, and answer key (pages 58–61)

⊙ dictionary

⊙ pencils

Extension Activity

Place two laminated copies of the number key in a center along with pencils, paper, and a timer. Invite student pairs to set a timer for a designated amount of time (such as five minutes) and then try to make as many words as possible by combining the prefixes and roots on the key. When time is up, have the partners compare their words and discuss the word meanings and uses. Direct students to check the dictionary for the meanings and spellings of any questionable words. If desired, have students work with additional Latin roots from the list on page 140.

Cube Words

Players: 2–4

Materials

- number key
- number cubes
- record sheet
- answer key
- dictionary
- pencils

1 Each student takes a record sheet and pencil.

2 To take a turn, roll both cubes.

- What number did the white cube land on? Find that number on the prefix section of the Cube Words Number Key. You will use this prefix to try to make a new word.

- What number did the gray cube land on? Find that number on the root section of the Cube Words number key. You will use one of these roots to try to make a new word.

3 Put the prefix together with each of the roots. Can you make at least one new word? If so, check the answer key to see if your word is correct.

- If your word is correct, go to step 4.

- If your word is not correct, your turn ends.

4 If you can make at least one word, write the word on your record sheet. (If you can make two words, choose only one word to write.) Then do the following:

- Tell what you think the word means (use the meanings on the key as clues). Look up the word in the dictionary. In your own words, write the meaning on your record sheet. Then draw an X in the box under "Dictionary Check" for that word.

- Give examples of how the word is used and use it in a sentence. Then draw an X in the box under "Use in Sentence" for that word.

5 Continue taking turns. The activity ends when a student fills in all of the lines on his or her record sheet. (Or continue until all students have filled in their record sheets).

Students may invite others to share what they know about the new words.

Cube Words Number Key

Number	1	2	3	4	5	6
Prefix	con (with)	ex (out)	in (in)	re (back)	sub (under)	trans (across, through)
Root	ceive (take)	clude (shut)	duct (lead)	ject (throw)	pose (place)	serve (save, keep)
Root	scribe (write)	mit (send)	port (carry)	tract (pull)	verse (turn)	struct (build)

Cube Words Number Cubes

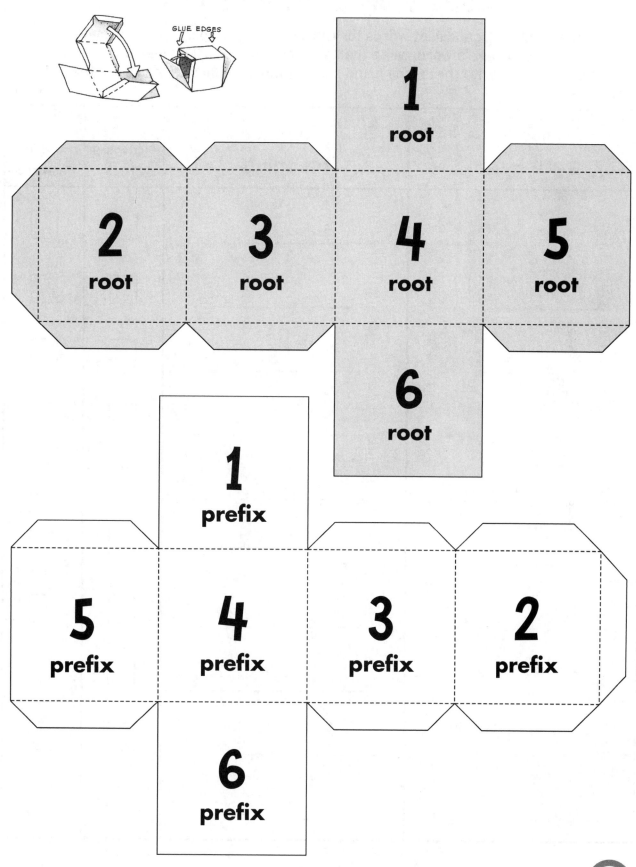

GLUE EDGES

1 root

2 root   **3** root   **4** root   **5** root

6 root

1 prefix

5 prefix   **4** prefix   **3** prefix   **2** prefix

6 prefix

Name: _____   Date: _____

Cube Words Record Sheet

Find the matching prefix and root words for the numbers you roll. If you can combine the prefix and a root to make a word, write that word on the line. Tell its meaning and check it in a dictionary. Then write the meaning and mark Dictionary Check. Finally, use the word in a sentence.

Word (prefix + root)	Word Meaning	Dictionary Check	Use in Sentence
1. _____	_____	☐	☐
2. _____	_____	☐	☐
3. _____	_____	☐	☐
4. _____	_____	☐	☐
5. _____	_____	☐	☐
6. _____	_____	☐	☐
7. _____	_____	☐	☐
8. _____	_____	☐	☐
9. _____	_____	☐	☐
_____	_____	☐	☐

con-

conceive

conclude

conduct

conserve

construct

contract

converse

re-

receive

reduct

reject

remit

report

repose

reserve

retract

reverse

ex-

exclude

export

expose

extract

sub-

subject

submit

subscribe

subtract

in-

include

induct

inject

inscribe

instruct

inverse

trans-

transmit

transport

transpose

transcribe

transverse

Go Greek!

Students make words by combining a variety of Greek prefixes and roots.

Players: 2–4, plus a word checker

Skill: Making words with Greek prefixes and roots

Getting Ready
Copy the Directions for Play. Copy and color four record sheets and one each of the word construction key and answer key. Laminate all game components.

Teaching Tips
Review the Greek prefixes and roots and their meanings before students play the game. Write a few examples of words that contain prefix-root or root-root combinations from the word construction key. Underline the Greek word parts in each word, tell their meanings, and discuss how they work together to make a word. Also, explain that some words are spelled by simply putting together two word parts, such as *paragraph*, *diagram*, and *astronaut*. But others, such as *dialogue*, *thermometer*, and *biology*, may have additional letters and syllables to account for the English spellings and pronunciations. Remind students about this as they work with the Greek prefixes and roots during the game.

Materials

- Directions for Play (page 63)
- Go Greek! record sheet, word construction key, and answer key (pages 64–66)
- coin
- wipe-off pens (one per player)
- dictionary

Extension Activity

Place a copy of the word construction key and answer key at a center, along with paper and pencils. Pair up students and have the partners work together to create words using word parts from the word construction key. Have students discuss the word meanings and their use. Then challenge the pair to use some of their words in a creative writing activity (such as in a letter, story, or play). Later, you might have students repeat the activity using Greek roots from the list on page 141.

Go Greek!

1. Each player takes a record sheet and wipe-off pen. The word checker takes the answer key.

2. To take a turn, toss the coin. If it lands on "heads," you get one chance to make a word. If it lands on "tails," you get two chances.

3. Start at Stone 1. Read the phrase under the blank line: prefix + root. These are the word parts you will need to make a word for that stone. Then do the following:

   - Choose different prefixes and roots on the word construction key. Use these word parts to try to form a word. Use the meanings on the key as a guide.

   - When you come up with a word, tell it to the other players.

4. Have the word checker check the answer key. If your word is on the key, write it on Stone 1. (The word checker can help you spell it.) Then follow these steps:

   - Tell what you think the word means. Look it up in the dictionary.

   - Give examples of how the word is used. Use the word in a sentence.

5. If you have two chances to make a word, and your word for Stone 1 was correct, go to Stone 2 and try to make a word. If the word for your first try was incorrect, try again to make a word for Stone 1.

6. Continue taking turns. The first player to fill in all the stones wins the game.

Players: 2–4, plus a word checker

Materials

- record sheet
- word construction key
- answer key
- coin
- wipe-off pens
- dictionary

- Players must fill in words on the stones in order from 1 to 10.

- Players may not repeat words on their game board.

Vocabulary Games & Activities That Boost Reading and Writing Skills © 2009 by Immacula A. Rhodes. Scholastic Teaching Resources

Record Sheet

Date: _____

**ord construction key to find two word parts that can be
er to make a word. Write the word on the line in the stone.**

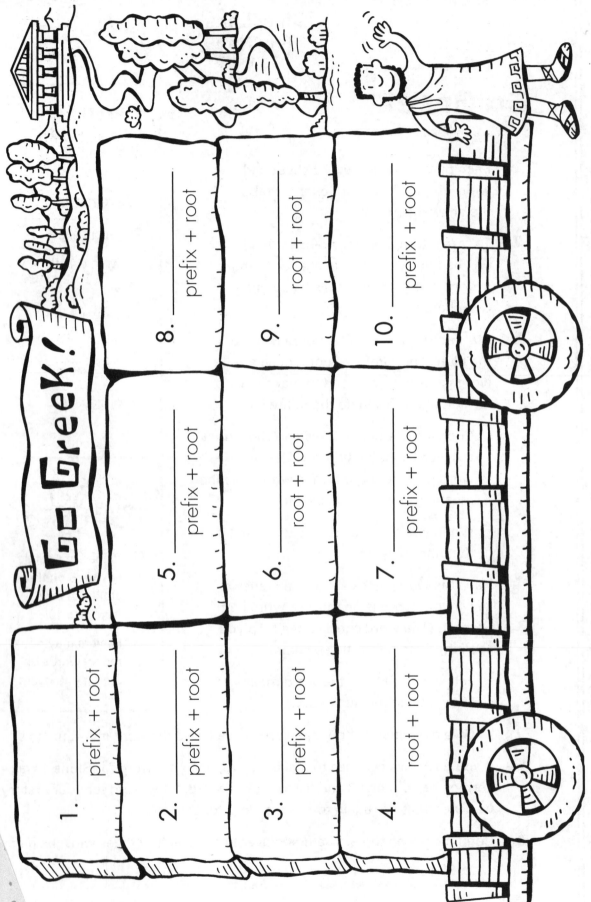

Go Greek!

1. _____
   prefix + root

2. _____
   prefix + root

3. _____
   prefix + root

4. _____
   root + root

5. _____
   prefix + root

6. _____
   root + root

7. _____
   prefix + root

8. _____
   prefix + root

9. _____
   root + root

10. _____
    prefix + root

Prefix	Root	Root
auto (self)	astro (star)	graph (written, drawn)
dia (through, across)	biblio (book)	log (idea, word, study)
homo (same, like)	bio (life)	meter (measure)
micro (small)	crat (rule)	naut (ship)
mono (one)	chron (time)	onym (name)
para (beside)	dem (people)	path (feeling, suffering)
peri (around)	geo (earth)	phon (sound, voice)
syn, sym (together)	gnos (to know)	scope (to see)
tele (far, distant)	gram (written, drawn)	therm (heat)

Note to Players: These are the most common words made by combining the Greek prefixes and roots in the game. Check a dictionary to see if other words are correct.

Prefix + Root		Root + Root	
autocrat	paragraph	astronaut	geography
autograph	parameter	bibliography	geology
diagnose	perimeter	biography	geometry
diagram	periscope	biology	geothermal
dialogue	symbiotic	biometric	gramophone
diameter	symmetry	chronograph	pathology
homograph	sympathy	chronology	phonogram
homonym	symphony	chronometer	phonograph
homophone	synchronize	democrat	phonology
microgram	synonym	demographic	thermometer
micrograph	telegram		
micrometer	telegraph		
microphone	telemeter		
microscope	telepathy		
monogram	telephone		
monograph	telescope		
monologue			

Synonym Scout

**Students explore word meanings
by matching synonyms.**

Players: 2

Skill: Identifying synonyms

Getting Ready

Copy the Directions for Play, game board, game
cards, and answer key. Color the game board.
Laminate all game components, then cut apart
the cards.

Teaching Tips

Before introducing the game, review synonyms
with students. Help them brainstorm a list of
synonym pairs. Then use one word in each pair
in a sentence. Have students repeat the sentence,
replacing the word with its synonym. Discuss
whether or not the replacement word changes the
meaning of the sentence, and, if so, how. Finally,
tell students that in the game, each word on the
game board has two synonym word cards that
go with it.

**Extension
Activities**

- Distribute copies of the answer key to students.
  Ask them to write additional synonyms on
  and around the rock for each word. Then have
  students compare their list of synonyms with
  classmates. They can use a thesaurus (or
  dictionary) to check their synonyms. Students
  can also write sentences using the bold words
  on the rocks and then share their sentences
  with partners, replacing these words with some
  of their own synonyms.

- To provide practice with a new set of words,
  mask the words on the game board and create
  a new set of word cards.

Synonym Scout

1 Each player takes a set of markers. Shuffle the cards and stack them facedown.

2 To play, toss the coin. If it lands on "heads," take one card. If it lands on "tails," take two cards.

3 Read the word on the card. If you can find a synonym for the word on the game board, name it. Check the answer key (or use a thesaurus or dictionary).

- If your answer is correct, place a marker on the rock and keep the card. Then give an example of how both words can be used as synonyms.

- If the answer is not correct, or if you cannot find a match on the game board, place the card on the bottom of the stack.

- If you took two cards, repeat step 3 with the other card.

4 Continue taking turns until all the rocks are covered with markers. The player with the most markers on the game board wins.

Players: 2

Materials

- ⊙ game boards
- ⊙ game cards
- ⊙ answer key
- ⊙ coin
- ⊙ thesaurus
- ⊙ dictionary

Players may not put their marker on a rock that is already covered by another player's marker.

Variation

In this version, each player tries to make a synonym match for every word on the game board. A player may cover a rock that holds the other player's marker, but not one that already holds his or her own marker. The first player to place one of his or her markers on all 15 rocks on the game board wins.

Synonym Scout

infant

argue

vehicle

music

soak

pretty

huge

youth

hurt

please

cruise

answer

sturdy

empty

tired

Synonym Scout Game Cards

Synonym Scout	Synonym Scout	Synonym Scout	Synonym Scout	Synonym Scout
adolescent	attractive	automobile	baby	beautiful
blank	car	damage	delight	drench
enormous	exhausted	fight	gigantic	harm
melody	newborn	powerful	quarrel	reply
respond	satisfy	strong	teenager	trip
tune	vacant	voyage	weary	wet

Vocabulary Games & Activities That Boost Reading and Writing Skills © 2009 by Immacula A. Rhodes. Scholastic Teaching Resources

Synonym Scout

Answer Key

argue
fight
quarrel

infant
baby
newborn

vehicle
automobile
car

music
melody
tune

soak
drench
wet

pretty
attractive
beautiful

huge
enormous
gigantic

youth
adolescent
teenager

hurt
damage
harm

please
delight
satisfy

cruise
trip
voyage

answer
reply
respond

sturdy
powerful
strong

empty
blank
vacant

tired
exhausted
weary

Antonym Aardvarks

Students use their word knowledge skills to find antonym pairs.

Players: Partners

Skill: Making antonym pairs

Getting Ready

Copy the Directions for Play, two sliders, and one of each set of word strips. Color the sliders. Laminate the Directions for Play, sliders, and word strips. Use the craft knife to cut the slits in the sliders. Cut apart the word strips. Insert one set of word strips (for example, both "A" strips) into one slider, and another set of strips in the other. Copy a supply of record sheets for players.

Teaching Tips

Review antonyms with students and help them brainstorm a list of antonym pairs. Then invite a volunteer to choose a word from the list and use it in a sentence. Ask another student to replace the word in the sentence with its antonym. Discuss with students how the antonym changes the sentence's meaning.

Materials

- Directions for Play (page 73)
- Antonym Aardvarks slider, word strips, record sheet, and answer key (pages 74–78)
- craft knife (for teacher use only)
- pencils

Extension Activities

- Write the words from this activity on separate index cards, or use antonym pairs of your own choice. Invite students to use the cards to play Antonym Concentration. Each time they make a match, have students explain the meaning of each word and give an example of its use.

- Use the word strips template (page 79) to create new antonym word strips. Students can create their own, too, and share them with the class.

Antonym Aardvarks

1 Each partner takes a slider, a record sheet, and pencil.

2 Slide your word strip to make the first word appear between the slits on the left. Then find the antonym for that word on the right strip.

3 Take turns reading aloud your word pairs. Discuss each word's meaning and give examples to show how each word is used. Then write the antonym pair on your record sheet. Continue taking turns in this way.

4 When you match and record all the antonym pairs, check the answer key. Place a check next to each correct pair and correct any errors.

5 To complete the record sheet, use one or both words in each antonym pair to write a sentence in the right column. Share your sentences with each other.

Players:
Partners

Materials

- ◉ Antonym Aardvarks slider
- ◉ word strips
- ◉ record sheet
- ◉ answer key
- ◉ pencils

- ◉ Players may talk about their word's meaning with each other and share examples of how the word is used.

- ◉ Players should fill in their record sheet from top to bottom, writing a different word pair in each section.

Antonym Aardvarks Slider

B	B	A	A
different	simple	rough	dull
cheap	narrow	strange	expert
complicated	friendly	terrible	gentle
wide	casual	brilliant	perfect
careless	similar	energetic	wonderful
deep	expensive	amateur	capture
formal	cautious	defective	normal
hostile	shallow	release	exhausted
B	B	A	A

D	content	silly	rude	damage
D	liquid	enormous	seldom	display
D	serious	random	panic	polite
D	unsafe	unhappy	fancy	calm
D	partial	allow	hide	often
D	tiny	solid	brief	ancient
D	orderly	total	repair	lengthy
D	forbid	secure	modern	plain

| D | | C | | C |

Name: _____ Date: _____

Antonym Aardvarks Record Sheet

Write each antonym pair. Check your pairs on the answer key. Check off or correct each pair. Then write a sentence with one or both words in each pair.

Antonyms	Sentence
☐ _____ ☐ _____	
☐ _____ ☐ _____	
☐ _____ ☐ _____	
☐ _____ ☐ _____	
☐ _____ ☐ _____	
☐ _____ ☐ _____	
☐ _____ ☐ _____	
☐ _____ ☐ _____	

Slider A

dull, brilliant

expert, amateur

gentle, rough

perfect, defective

wonderful, terrible

capture, release

normal, strange

exhausted, energetic

Slider C

damage, repair

display, hide

polite, rude

calm, panic

often, seldom

ancient, modern

lengthy, brief

plain, fancy

Slider B

simple, complicated

narrow, wide

friendly, hostile

casual, formal

similar, different

expensive, cheap

cautious, careless

shallow, deep

Slider D

silly, serious

enormous, tiny

random, orderly

unhappy, content

allow, forbid

solid, liquid

total, partial

secure, unsafe

Antonym Aardvarks Word Strips Template

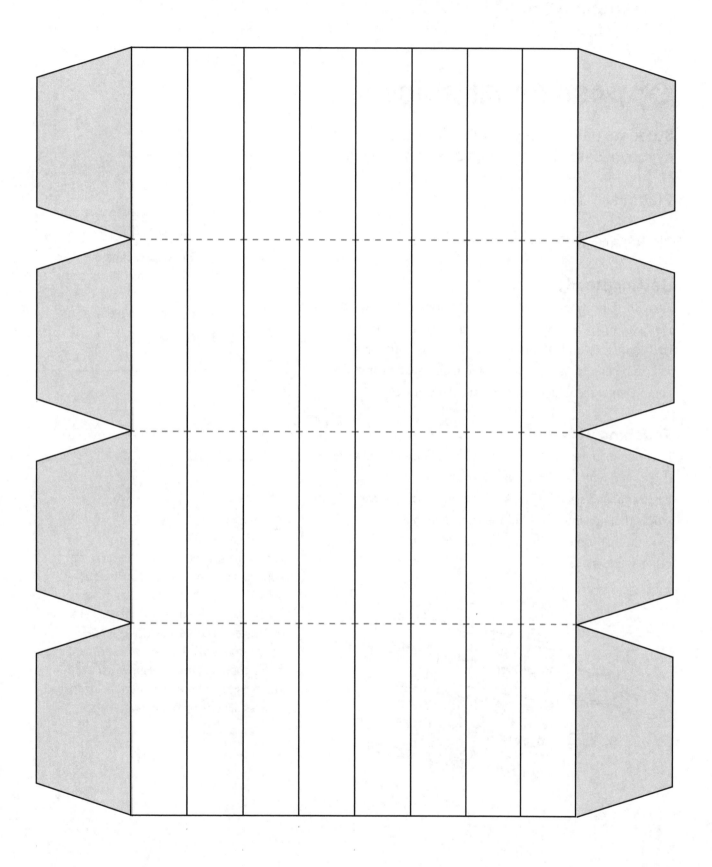

Opposites Attract

Students pair synonym sets with other synonym sets that are opposite in meaning.

Players: 2–4

Skill: Sorting synonyms and antonyms

Getting Ready
Copy the Directions for Play. Make two copies of the word mat page (there are two mats per page) and one each of the word cards and answer key. Number the word mats 1–4, and color each a different color. Laminate all game components, then cut apart the mats and game cards.

Teaching Tips
Review synonyms and antonyms with students. Then write three synonyms on chart paper or a whiteboard, such as *hot, warm,* and *steamy.* Have students brainstorm three words that are antonyms (for instance, *cold, chilly,* and *icy*). Explain that some synonym sets can be the opposite of other synonym sets.

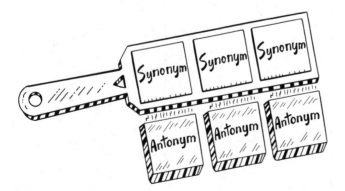

Materials

- Directions for Play (page 81)

- Opposites Attract word mats, word cards, and answer key (pages 82–85)

- thesaurus

Extension Activity

For an interesting twist, use the activity to help students make word associations. First mask all the text on a copy of a word mat and copy the mat several times. Then create sets of six word cards, each labeled with words that are associated in some way (for example, *house, condominium, trailer, apartment, houseboat,* and *ranch*). Finally, invite students to sort the words—grouping them by association—onto the word mats.

Opposites Attract

Players: 2–4

Materials

- ◉ word mats
- ◉ word cards
- ◉ answer key
- ◉ thesaurus

1 Spread out Word Mats 1, 2, 3, and 4. Shuffle the cards and stack them facedown. Place the top card on Word Mat 1, on a "magnet" space.

2 The first player takes the next card. The player reads the word, then does one of the following:

- If the word on the card is a synonym for the first word: The player places the card on Word Mat 1, on a new "magnet" (synonym) space.

- If the word on the card is an antonym for the first word: The player places the card on Word Mat 1, on a "steel bar" (antonym).

- If neither: The player places the card on Word Mat 2, on a magnet space.

3 Players take turns placing cards on the mats in this way. The player reads the new word, then does one of the following:

- If the word is a synonym for a word on a magnet: The player places the card on that magnet.

- If the word is an antonym for a word on a magnet: The player places the card on the steel bar below that magnet.

- If a synonym or antonym for the word is not already on a mat: The player places the card on the magnet of a new mat.

4 Play continues until all of the cards have been used. When finished, players check each mat:

- The three words on each magnet should be synonyms.

- The three words on each set of steel bars should be antonyms of the words on the magnets.

- ◉ Players may talk about their word's meaning with each other and share examples of how the word is used.

- ◉ Each of the three words on the steel bars will be synonyms for each other.

Vocabulary Games & Activities That Boost Reading and Writing Skills © 2009 by Immacula A. Rhodes. Scholastic Teaching Resources

Word Mat # _____

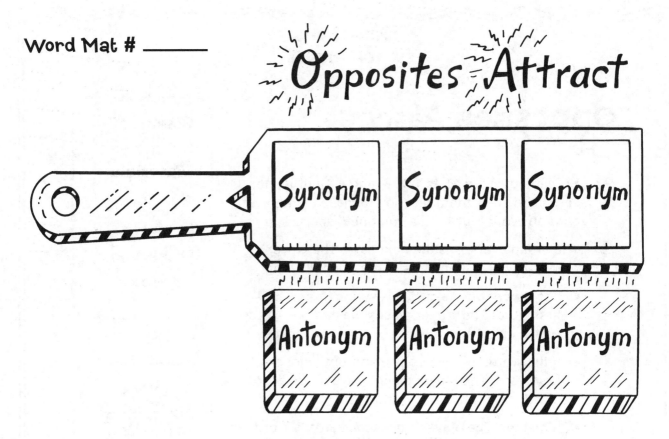

Word Mat # _____

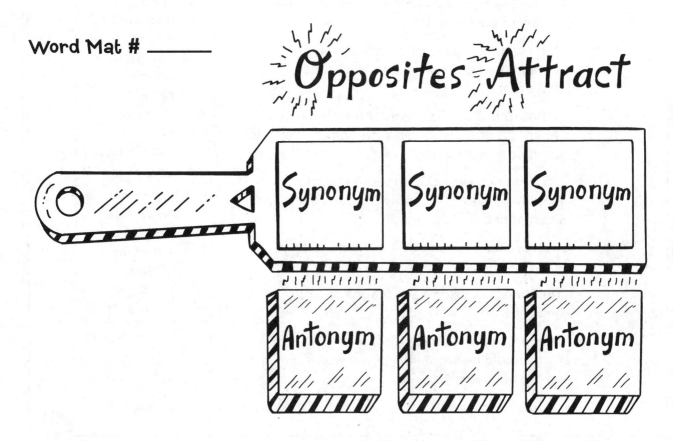

Opposites Attract Game Cards

begin	buddy	cheerful	complicated
proceed	companion	content	difficult
start	friend	happy	hard
conclude	enemy	dejected	basic
end	foe	depressed	easy
finish	rival	sad	simple

Opposites Attract Game Cards

enormous	hush	narrow	race
huge	peace	slender	rush
large	quiet	thin	speed
miniature	chaos	broad	crawl
small	commotion	vast	creep
tiny	noise	wide	inch

Antonyms

Synonyms	**Synonyms**
begin	end
start	finish
proceed	conclude

Antonyms

Synonyms	**Synonyms**
happy	sad
cheerful	dejected
content	depressed

Antonyms

Synonyms	**Synonyms**
narrow	broad
slender	vast
thin	wide

Antonyms

Synonyms	**Synonyms**
hard	easy
difficult	simple
complicated	basic

Antonyms

Synonyms	**Synonyms**
large	small
huge	tiny
enormous	miniature

Antonyms

Synonyms	**Synonyms**
friend	foe
buddy	enemy
companion	rival

Antonyms

Synonyms	**Synonyms**
hush	noise
quiet	commotion
peace	chaos

Antonyms

Synonyms	**Synonyms**
speed	creep
race	crawl
rush	inch

Double-Duty Words

Students use multiple-meaning words to represent different parts of speech.

Players: 2–3

Skill: Using multiple-meaning words (homographs)

Getting Ready

Copy the Directions for Play, game board, each set of game cards (use a different color paper for each set: Double-Duty cards and Triple! cards), and a supply of score sheets. Color the game board and score sheets. Laminate all game components, then cut apart the cards and score sheets.

Teaching Tips

Explain that some words are spelled and pronounced alike, but have multiple meanings. Many of these words can be both nouns (naming words) and verbs (action words). Some can also be adjectives or adverbs. Name some multiple-meaning words (such as *ride, bat, grade, right,* and *drink*), use them in sentences, and discuss what part of speech they represent and why. Invite students to brainstorm other examples of multiple-meaning words and provide examples of their different meanings.

Materials

- Directions for Play (page 87)
- Double-Duty Words game board, game cards, and score sheet (pages 88–91)
- coin
- game markers (such as buttons or counters, each a different color; one per player)
- wipe-off pens (one per player)
- dictionary

Extension Activity

Display a list of multiple-meaning words at a center for small groups to use in the following activity. To begin, have a student choose a word from the list, keeping it a secret from the group. Have the student give clues about the word, including clues that represent different uses of the word. (For example, for *bat,* the student might say, "This is used to hit a ball, but it can also hang upside down in caves.") Challenge the group to guess the word and then suggest other ways to describe the different meanings of the word without using the actual word.

Double-Duty Words

Players: 2–3

Materials

- ◉ game board
- ◉ game cards
- ◉ score sheet
- ◉ coin
- ◉ game markers
- ◉ wipe-off pens
- ◉ dictionary

1 Shuffle the "Double-Duty" cards and the "Triple!" cards. Stack each set facedown.

2 Each player takes a score sheet, a wipe-off pen, and a game marker. Players place their game markers on Start.

3 To take a turn, toss the coin. If it lands on "heads," move one space. If it lands on "tails," move two spaces. Follow the directions on the space. If the space is marked **Noun**, **Verb**, or **Triple!**, follow these directions:

- Noun or Verb: Take the Double-Duty card on top. Read the word, and use it as that part of speech in a sentence.

- Triple!: Take the Triple! card on top. Read the word, then use three different meanings of the word in sentences. You can use the word as a noun or verb.

4 Check a dictionary to find out if you used the word correctly. You can also check with other players.

- If you are correct, write the word on your score sheet. Draw an X in the box for Noun, Verb, or Triple! to show how you used the word. Use the key to find out your points. Write the points in the box. Then set the card aside.

- If you are not correct, place the card on the bottom of the stack.

5 Continue taking turns. When all players reach Finish, they add their points. The player with the most points wins.

- ◉ Keep in mind:
  - A noun names a person, place, or thing.
  - A verb names an action.

- ◉ Players may invite others to share ways to use the word as different parts of speech.

Game Board

Double-Duty Words

Fly-Boy

Start

Noun

Verb

Skip a turn.

Noun

Noun

Triple!

Verb

Take another turn.

Verb

Noun

Verb

Triple!

Finish

Verb

Noun

Double-Duty Cards

Move ahead 1 space.

Triple! Cards

Verb

Noun

Triple!

Verb

Noun

Move back 1 space.

Verb

Noun

Double-Duty Words Game Cards

lie	duck	fly	report
hit	saw	step	pet
hammer	pad	pool	punch
rear	waste	root	shed
sock	soil	sign	steer
stoop	tire	toast	rip

Double-Duty Words Game Cards

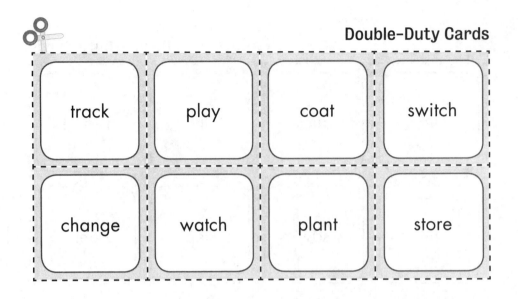

track	play	coat	switch
change	watch	plant	store

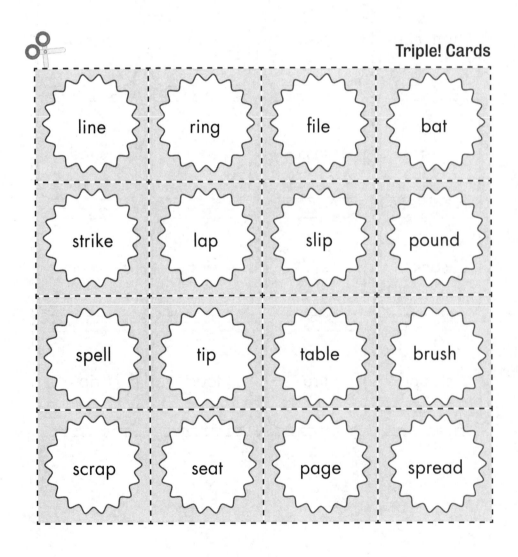

line	ring	file	bat
strike	lap	slip	pound
spell	tip	table	brush
scrap	seat	page	spread

Vocabulary Games & Activities That Boost Reading and Writing Skills © 2009 by Immacula A. Rhodes. Scholastic Teaching Resources

Name: _____ Date: _____

Double-Duty Words Score Sheet

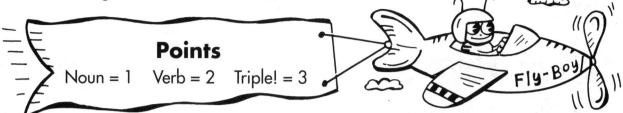

Points

Noun = 1   Verb = 2   Triple! = 3

Use the word on your card in a sentence. Then write the word, check off the part of speech, and fill in the points. Add all your points at the end of the game.

Word	Part of Speech	Points	Word	Part of Speech	Points
	_____ Noun _____ Verb _____ Triple!			_____ Noun _____ Verb _____ Triple!	
	_____ Noun _____ Verb _____ Triple!			_____ Noun _____ Verb _____ Triple!	
	_____ Noun _____ Verb _____ Triple!			_____ Noun _____ Verb _____ Triple!	
	_____ Noun _____ Verb _____ Triple!			_____ Noun _____ Verb _____ Triple!	
	_____ Noun _____ Verb _____ Triple!			_____ Noun _____ Verb _____ Triple!	
	_____ Noun _____ Verb _____ Triple!			_____ Noun _____ Verb _____ Triple!	
	_____ Noun _____ Verb _____ Triple!			_____ Noun _____ Verb _____ Triple!	
	_____ Noun _____ Verb _____ Triple!			_____ Noun _____ Verb _____ Triple!	
	Total Points				

Analogy Galaxy

Students explore meanings and relationships of words to complete analogies.

Players: 2–3

Skill: Completing analogies

Getting Ready

Copy the Directions for Play, game board, game cards, markers, and answer key. Color the game board. Laminate all game components, then cut apart the game cards and markers.

Teaching Tips

Explain that solving analogies helps students analyze the relationship between two pairs of words and can help them learn new words. When working with analogies, they need to think about the definitions and uses of key words in the construct. Brainstorm several analogies with students, encouraging them to explain the relationship represented in each example. (You might use a "think-aloud" method to model how you devised a few examples.) As you work, guide students to suggest analogies that show different types of relationships, such as:

- part to whole (**Water** is to **lake** as **sand** is to **desert**.)

- comparisons (**Mouse** is to **small** as **elephant** is to **big**.)

- antonyms (**Fast** is to **slow** as **happy** is to **sad**.)

- synonyms (**Quick** is to **fast** as **humorous** is to **funny**.)

- object to use (**Pen** is to **write** as **shovel** is to **dig**.)

- item to category (**Strawberry** is to **fruit** as **broccoli** is to **vegetable**.)

You may also want to introduce other analogy formats students may encounter—for example:

strawberry: **fruit** :: **broccoli**: **vegetable**

Materials

- Directions for Play (page 93)
- Analogy Galaxy game board, game cards, game markers, and answer key (pages 94–99)
- coin

Extension Activity

Provide a list of word pairs in which a relationship can be identified between the words in a pair. Challenge students to choose five word pairs and write analogies for them. For example, for *sun/day*, a student might write, "Sun is to day as moon is to night." When finished, invite students to share and compare their analogies. Discuss the different relationships students identify for each word pair.

Analogy Galaxy

1 Stack two game markers above (or next to) the word on each planet on the game board. (Make sure the word is not covered.) Shuffle the cards and stack them facedown.

2 To take a turn, toss the coin.

- If it lands on "heads," take one card and read the analogy. Search the planets for the word that completes the analogy. Read the completed analogy aloud, and explain your answer.

- If it lands on "tails," take two cards. Read the first analogy. Search the planets for the word that completes the analogy. Read the completed analogy aloud, and explain your answer. Repeat for the second card.

3 After completing each analogy, check the answer key. Is your answer correct?

- If so, take a marker off that planet and keep the analogy card.

- If not, place the card on the bottom of the stack.

4 Continue taking turns until all the markers have been removed from the planets. The player with the most markers wins the game.

Players: 2–3

Materials

- ⊙ game board
- ⊙ game cards
- ⊙ game markers
- ⊙ answer key
- ⊙ coin

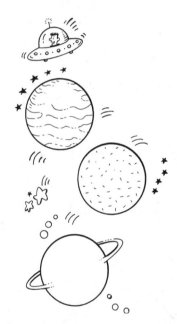

There are two analogy cards for the word on each planet.

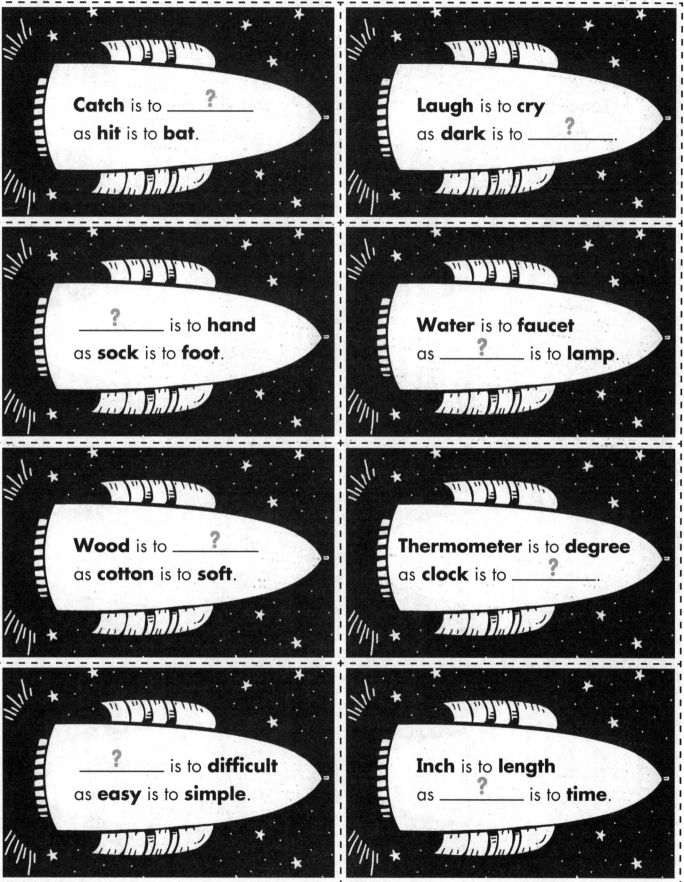

Catch is to _____ **?**
as **hit** is to **bat**.

Laugh is to **cry**
as **dark** is to _____ **?**.

_____ **?** is to **hand**
as **sock** is to **foot**.

Water is to **faucet**
as _____ **?** is to **lamp**.

Wood is to _____ **?**
as **cotton** is to **soft**.

Thermometer is to **degree**
as **clock** is to _____ **?**.

_____ **?** is to **difficult**
as **easy** is to **simple**.

Inch is to **length**
as _____ **?** is to **time**.

Tooth is to _____ **?**
as **room** is to **house**.

Artist is to **paintbrush**
as **author** is to _____ **?**.

Nose is to **smell**
as _____ **?** is to **talk**.

_____ **?** is to **write**
as **scissors** is to **cut**.

Bench is to _____ **?**
as **desk** is to **school**.

Wing is to _____ **?**
as **wheel** is to **bus**.

_____ **?** is to **drive**
as **stop** is to **go**.

Train is to **engineer**
as _____ **?** is to **pilot**.

Fly is to **insect** as **flower** is to ___?___.

Three is to **number** as **square** is to ___?___.

___?___ is to **farmer** as **teach** is to **teacher**.

Blanket is to **cover** as ___?___ is to **form**.

Sad is to **blue** as **anger** is to ___?___.

Lamb is to ___?___ as **bear** is to **cub**.

Yellow is to **banana** as ___?___ is to **apple**.

Milk is to **cow** as ___?___ is to **wool**.

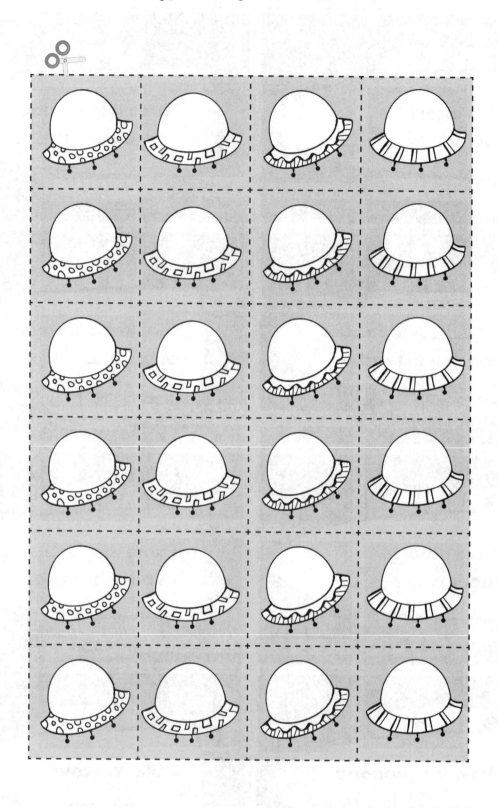

Glove:

Catch is to **glove** as **hit** is to **bat**.

Glove is to **hand** as **sock** is to **foot**.

Hard:

Wood is to **hard** as **cotton** is to **soft**.

Hard is to **difficult** as
easy is to **simple**.

Light:

Laugh is to **cry** as **dark** is to **light**.

Water is to **faucet** as
light is to **lamp**.

Minute:

Temperature is to **degree** as
clock is to **minute**.

Inch is to **length** as **minute**
is to **time**.

Mouth:

Tooth is to **mouth** as
room is to **house**.

Nose is to **smell** as **mouth** is to **talk**.

Park:

Bench is to **park** as
desk is to **school**.

Park is to **drive** as **stop** is to **go**.

Pencil:

Artist is to **paintbrush** as
author is to **pencil**.

Pencil is to **write** as
scissors is to **cut**.

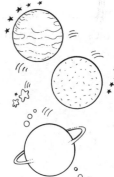

Plane:

Wing is to **plane** as **wheel** is to **bus**.

Train is to **engineer** as
plane is to **pilot**.

Plant:

Fly is to **insect** as **flower** is to **plant**.

Plant is to **farmer** as
teach is to **teacher**.

Red:

Sad is to **blue** as **anger** is to **red**.

Yellow is to **banana** as
red is to **apple**.

Shape:

Three is to **number** as
square is to **shape**.

Blanket is to **cover** as
shape is to **form**.

Sheep:

Lamb is to **sheep** as **bear** is to **cub**.

Cow is to **milk** as **sheep** is to **wool**.

Heteronym Hive

Students use the different pronunciations and meanings of various heteronyms in sentences.

Players: 2

Skill: Using heteronyms

Getting Ready

Copy the Directions for Play, game board, game cards, and answer key. Color the game board. Laminate all game components, then cut apart the game cards.

Teaching Tips

Before playing the game, explain that heteronyms are a type of homograph—they are words that are spelled the same, but are pronounced differently depending on how they are used. Share a few examples of heteronyms, such as *drawer*, *desert*, and *suspect*, giving the meaning represented by each pronunciation and using them in sentences. Encourage students to brainstorm and give examples of other heteronyms they are familiar with.

Materials

- Directions for Play (page 101)
- Heteronym Hive game boards, game cards, and answer key (pages 102–107)
- coin
- dictionary

Extension Activities

- To convert the game to an independent center activity, copy and laminate the game pieces. Cut apart the game cards and each beehive cell that is labeled with a word. Invite students to sort the sentences by matching each one to the word that best completes it. When finished, have students check their answers on the answer key.

- To make a new game, mask the words on a game board and program it with a new set of heteronyms (see page 142). Create a new set of game cards to match (see game cards template, page 106).

Heteronym Hive

Players: 2

Materials
- ◉ game boards
- ◉ game cards
- ◉ answer key
- ◉ coin
- ◉ dictionary

1 Each player chooses a game board. Shuffle the cards and stack them facedown.

2 To take a turn, toss the coin.

- If it lands on "heads," take one card. Read the sentence aloud. Search your game board for a word that completes the sentence. If you find one, read the completed sentence and explain your answer.

- If it lands on "tails," take two cards. Read the first sentence. Search your game board for a word that completes the sentence. If you find one, read the completed sentence, and explain your answer. Repeat for the second card.

3 After completing each sentence, check the answer key.

- If your answer is correct, match the bee to one of the black "holes" along the edge of that word cell.

- If your answer is not correct, place the card at the bottom of the stack.

4 Continue taking turns. The first player to match bees to all of the holes on his or her game board wins. (Or continue playing until both players have matched all the bees and holes.)

Playing Tips

- ◉ There are two cards for each word cell on a game board. Keep in mind that each time a word is used, it will have a different meaning and pronunciation.

- ◉ Players may use a dictionary to check the pronunciation or meaning of their word.

Heteronym Hive Game Board

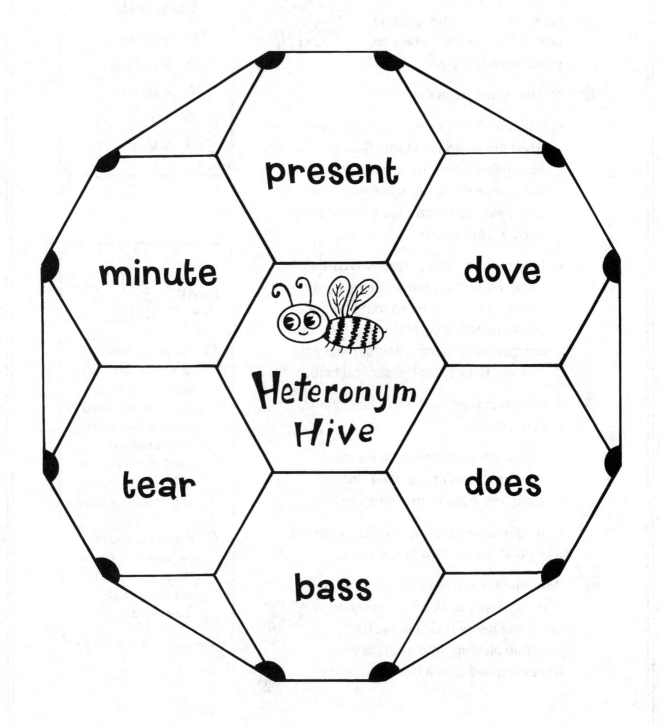

present

minute

dove

Heteronym Hive

tear

does

bass

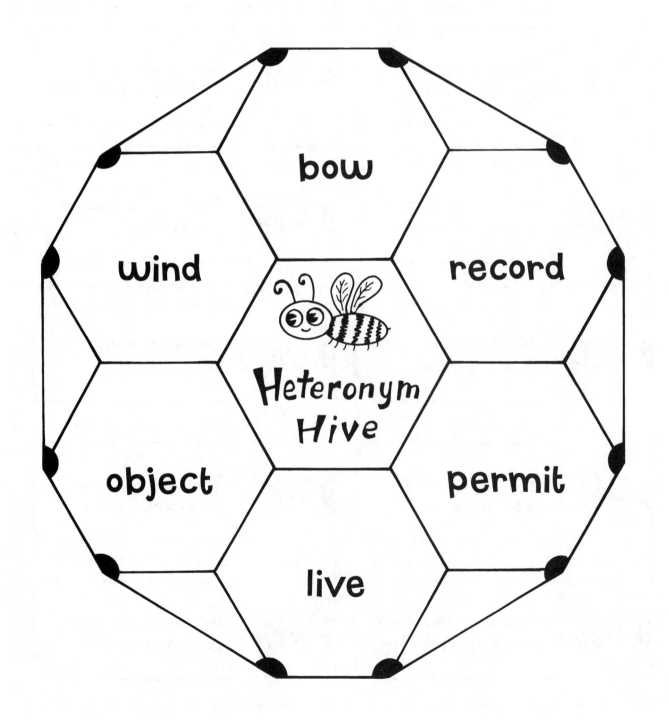

bow

wind

record

Heteronym Hive

object

permit

live

Heteronym Hive Game Cards

 My dad sings _____ with his singing group.

 Joe caught a small _____ on our fishing trip.

 Two _____ ran quickly into the forest.

 How _____ an airplane stay up the sky?

 Vic _____ into the deep end of the pool.

 A white _____ flew over the tree.

 Our class will _____ a gift to the principal.

 Mary gave me a _____ for my birthday.

 A _____ is the same as 60 seconds.

 That spot is so _____ I can barely see it.

 A _____ rolled slowly down the sad boy's face.

 Did you _____ your pants when you fell?

Vocabulary Games & Activities That Boost Reading and Writing Skills © 2009 by Immacula A. Rhodes. Scholastic Teaching Resources

Heteronym Hive Game Cards

 Pam tied a blue _____ around the gift.

 The dancers took a _____ at the end of the show.

 Three cats _____ in our barn.

 Is that a _____ or a silk flower?

 There is a strange _____ floating in my cup.

 I heard a man _____ to closing the pool early.

 My brother just got his learner's _____ to drive.

 Dad will not _____ us to ride our bikes across town.

 The band met to _____ their new song.

 Mia broke the _____ for reading the most books.

 Please _____ the kite string around the spool.

The _____ blew the leaves across the yard.

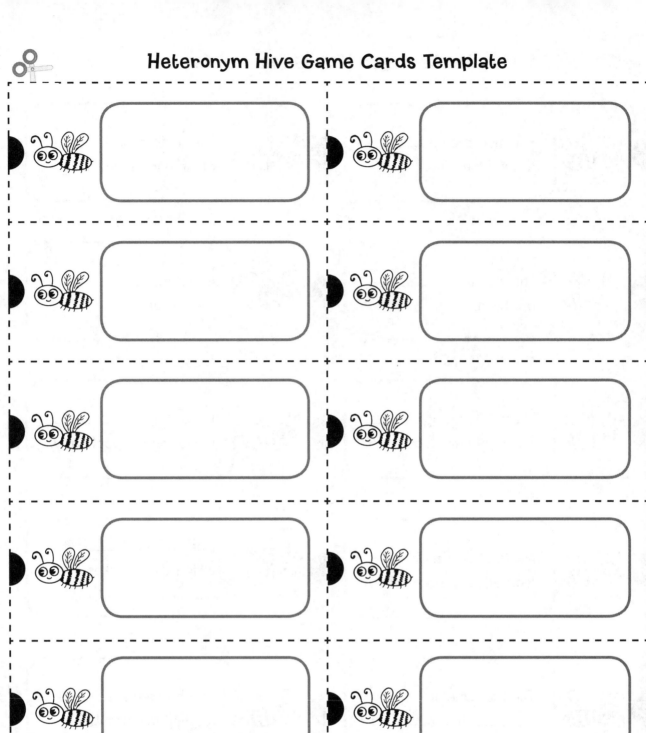

bass

My dad sings <u>bass</u> with his singing group.

Joe caught a small <u>bass</u> on our fishing trip.

bow

Pam tied a blue <u>bow</u> around the gift.

The dancers took a <u>bow</u> at the end of the show.

does

Two <u>does</u> ran quickly into the forest.

How <u>does</u> an airplane stay up the sky?

dove

Vic <u>dove</u> into the deep end of the pool.

A white <u>dove</u> flew over the tree.

live

Three cats <u>live</u> in our barn.

Is that a <u>live</u> or a silk flower?

minute

A <u>minute</u> is the same as 60 seconds.

That spot is so <u>minute</u> I can barely see it.

object

There is a strange <u>object</u> floating in my cup.

I heard a man <u>object</u> to closing the pool early.

permit

My brother just got his learner's <u>permit</u> to drive.

Dad will not <u>permit</u> us to ride our bikes across town.

present

Our class will <u>present</u> a gift to the principal.

Mary gave me a <u>present</u> for my birthday.

record

The band met to <u>record</u> their new song.

Mia broke the <u>record</u> for reading the most books.

tear

A <u>tear</u> rolled slowly down the sad boy's face.

Did you <u>tear</u> your pants when you fell?

wind

Please <u>wind</u> the kite string around the spool.

The <u>wind</u> blew the leaves across the yard.

Vocabulary Games & Activities That Boost Reading and Writing Skills © 2009 by Immacula A. Rhodes. Scholastic Teaching Resources

Deal & Draw

Students use picture clues to identify homophone pairs.

Players: 2–5

Skill: Identifying homophones

Getting Ready

Copy the Directions for Play, a supply of record sheets, and a set of game cards. Laminate all game components, then cut apart the cards. Place a basket of pencils or crayons with the easel (or clipboard) for this activity.

Teaching Tips

Before students play, review the homophone pairs on the cards with them. Discuss the meaning of each word in a pair. Point out any possible differences in pronunciation, such as with the words *aunt* and *clothes*. Then invite students to use the words in sentences.

Materials

- Directions for Play (page 109)
- Deal and Draw record sheet and game cards (pages 110–113)
- wipe-off pens (one per player)
- basket of pencils or crayons
- supply of drawing paper
- easel or clipboard
- kitchen timer

Extension Activity

Instead of drawing pictures, challenge players to verbally describe one of the words on their card—without using the actual word. As other players guess the word, have them write it on their record sheets in the space designated for the picture. Then have them write the homophone in the space under the word. Afterward, players can look at the word card to check their answers.

Deal & Draw

1 Each player takes a record sheet, wipe-off pen, and sheet of drawing paper. Players write the names of other players at the top of their record sheet, but not their own name.

2 One player shuffles the cards and stacks them facedown.

3 The first player to take a turn selects the top card and reads the words but doesn't share them with the other players. This player clips a sheet of drawing paper to the easel and chooses one of the words to draw.

4 The player sets a timer to three minutes then starts drawing a picture to represent the word. The other players try to guess the word.

5 As players guess the word, they find the drawer's name on their record sheet. They fill in the box below that name as follows:

- Write the word for the picture in the top section of the first box.

- Write a homophone for the word in the bottom section of that box.

Note: If no player correctly guesses the word, go to step 7.

6 When the timer goes off, the drawer shows the card, and reads and spells the word. The players who guessed the word make any needed corrections to their record sheet.

7 Players take turns choosing a new card and selecting a word to draw. Players repeat steps 4–6 each time.

Players: 2–5

Materials

- ◉ record sheet
- ◉ wipe-off pens
- ◉ drawing paper
- ◉ game cards
- ◉ easel or clipboard
- ◉ kitchen timer
- ◉ pencils or crayons

- ◉ To save paper, students may fold their drawing paper in half and use a blank section of the paper on each turn to draw their picture.

- ◉ For the first round of drawings, students fill in the top row of boxes. Then they move down one row at a time to fill in the boxes for rounds 2, 3, and 4.

Vocabulary Games & Activities That Boost Reading and Writing Skills © 2009 by Immacula A. Rhodes. Scholastic Teaching Resources

Name: _____

Date: _____

Deal & Draw Record Sheet

Guess what the player is drawing. Write the name of the picture in the top half of a box under the player's name. Write the homophone for the word in the bottom half of the box.

Player:				
picture word 〜〜〜〜 homophone	〜〜〜〜	〜〜〜〜	〜〜〜〜	〜〜〜〜
picture word 〜〜〜〜 homophone	〜〜〜〜	〜〜〜〜	〜〜〜〜	〜〜〜〜
picture word 〜〜〜〜 homophone	〜〜〜〜	〜〜〜〜	〜〜〜〜	〜〜〜〜
picture word 〜〜〜〜 homophone	〜〜〜〜	〜〜〜〜	〜〜〜〜	〜〜〜〜

Vocabulary Games & Activities That Boost Reading and Writing Skills © 2009 by Immacula A. Rhodes. Scholastic Teaching Resources (page 110)

Deal & Draw	Deal & Draw	Deal & Draw
ad add	ant aunt	ate eight
ball bawl	bare bear	be bee
beat beet	berry bury	board bored
brake break	cereal serial	close clothes
creak creek	crews cruise	cymbal symbol

Deal & Draw	Deal & Draw	Deal & Draw
dear deer	doe dough	eye I
fairy ferry	flea flee	flour flower
hair hare	hall haul	hear here
hoarse horse	hoes hose	knight night
made maid	mail male	one won

Deal & Draw

pail
pale

Deal & Draw

pair
pear

Deal & Draw

plain
plane

Deal & Draw

sail
sale

Deal & Draw

sea
see

Deal & Draw

son
sun

Deal & Draw

stairs
stares

Deal & Draw

stake
steak

Deal & Draw

tail
tale

Deal & Draw

tea
tee

Deal & Draw

throne
thrown

Deal & Draw

toe
tow

Deal & Draw

wail
whale

Deal & Draw

waist
waste

Deal & Draw

weak
week

Compound Word Climb

Students combine words to create compound words.

Players: 2

Skill: Building compound words

Getting Ready

Copy the Directions for Play. Make two copies of the record sheet, and one copy each of the game board, game cards, markers, and reference key. Color the game board and markers. Laminate all game components, then cut apart the cards and markers. Place the game cards in a resealable sandwich bag.

Teaching Tips

Review compound words with students. Then read the word on each game card. Ask students to brainstorm a few compound words using each word as the first part (for example, *backyard*) and then as the last part (for example, *comeback*).

Materials

- ◉ Directions for Play (page 115)
- ◉ Compound Word Climb game board, record sheet, game markers, game cards, and reference key (pages 116–119)
- ◉ resealable sandwich bag
- ◉ wipe-off pens (one per player)
- ◉ dictionary

Extension Activities

- ◉ Challenge students' word-building skills and help them make associations with this activity. First, have one student in a pair name a compound word, such as *nightlight*. Ask his or her partner to name a compound word that begins with the last part of that word (such as *lighthouse*). Have the partners take turns adding words to make as long a compound word chain as possible (for example, *housetop, topsail, sailboat, boatyard, yardstick, stickball,* and *ballpark*).

- ◉ Use the blank word cards (page 118) to add new words to the game.

Compound Word Climb

1 Each player takes a record sheet, wipe-off pen, and game marker. Players place their game markers on Start.

2 Draw a card from the bag. Read the word aloud and write it on the Starter Word line on your record sheet.

- Think of a compound word using your word as the first small word in the new word.

- Say the new word and explain its meaning. Give an example of its use, then write the word on line 1 on the left.

- Move your game marker to step 1.

3 On your next turn, find the last small word in the compound word on line 1. Can you use it as the first small word in a new compound word?

- Yes: Say the new word. Write it on line 2 on the left. Move your game marker to step 2.

- No: Try to use the first small word in the compound word on line 1 to make another compound word. Write it on line 1 on the right. Leave your game marker on step 1.

4 On your last turn, did you write a word on the left or right line?

- Left Line: Repeat step 3 on your next turn.

- Right Line: Look at the last small word in the compound word. Can you use that word as the first small word in a new compound word? If so, write the new word on the next line up on the left. If not, you "fall off" the wall and must start your climb again. Erase your record sheet and draw a new card on your next turn.

5 Continue taking turns. The first player to move a marker to End wins.

Players: 2

Materials

- ⊙ game board
- ⊙ record sheet
- ⊙ game cards
- ⊙ game markers
- ⊙ reference key
- ⊙ wipe-off pens
- ⊙ dictionary

Players may share what they know about the compound words.

Vocabulary Games & Activities That Boost Reading and Writing Skills © 2009 by Immacula A. Rhodes. Scholastic Teaching Resources

Game Board

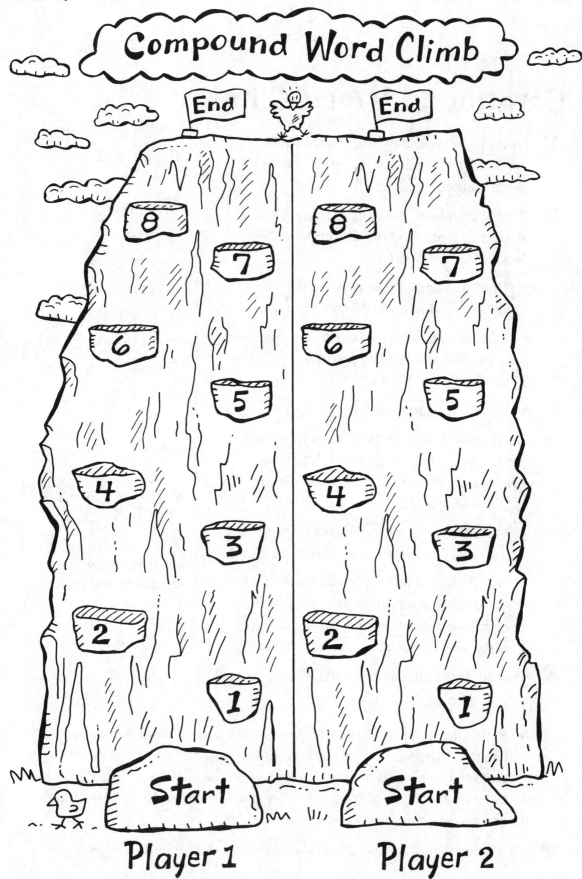

Compound Word Climb

Name: _____   Date: _____

Write a compound word for each number. Use the Starter Word in your first compound word. Follow the game directions to fill in the other lines.

Compound Word Climb

End Word: _____

8. _____   _____

7. _____   _____

6. _____   _____

5. _____   _____

4. _____   _____

3. _____   _____

2. _____   _____

1. _____   _____

Starter Word: _____

Game Markers

back	ball	bed	boat
book	car	day	down
fire	hand	head	horse
house	land	out	side
stick	time	top	up
work			

Use this list to help you get started on your compound word climb. You can also use it to get ideas for compound words as you climb.

back

background	horseback
backspace	paperback
backyard	quarterback

ball

ballpark	baseball
ballplayer	football
ballroom	meatball

bed

bedroom	flowerbed
bedpost	sickbed
bedspread	waterbed

boat

boathouse	houseboat
boatload	sailboat
boatyard	rowboat

book

bookend	notebook
bookmark	schoolbook
bookshelf	workbook

car

carpool	boxcar
carport	racecar
carsick	sidecar

day

daydream	birthday
daylight	someday
daytime	weekday

down

download	breakdown
downtown	meltdown
downside	touchdown

fire

firefly	backfire
fireplace	campfire
firewood	surefire

hand

handbag	underhand
handcuff	offhand
handrail	beforehand

head

headroom	hardhead
headboard	arrowhead
headlight	overhead

horse

horsefly	seahorse
horseshoe	racehorse
horseplay	workhorse

house

houseguest	clubhouse
housekeeper	lighthouse
housework	warehouse

land

landfall	fairyland
landmark	homeland
landslide	wasteland

out

outdoor	carryout
outlast	lookout
outsmart	workout

slide

sideline	wayside
sidestep	bedside
sidetrack	waterside

stick

stickball	broomstick
stickpin	candlestick
stickup	lipstick

time

timeline	lifetime
timekeeper	nighttime
timetable	overtime

top

topcoat	blacktop
topsail	mountaintop
topsoil	rooftop

up

upset	makeup
upstream	pickup
uptight	roundup

work

workbench	footwork
workload	roadwork
workshop	homework

Onomatopoeia Bingo

Students explore words that represent sounds.

Players: 2–4

Skill: Identifying onomatopoeic words

Getting Ready

Copy the Directions for Play. Make four copies of the game board and one copy each of the spinner, arrow, and reference key. Color the spinner. Laminate all game components, then cut apart the spinner and arrow. Use the paper fastener to attach the arrow to the spinner.

Teaching Tips

Explain to students that onomatopoeic words are words that imitate or suggest sounds. Name some examples of these noise words, such as *buzz, hiss, pop, whoosh, hum,* and *click.* Invite students to name other noise words and tell what might make that noise or where they might hear it.

Materials

- Directions for Play (page 121)
- Onomatopoeia Bingo game board, spinner, arrow, and reference key (pages 122–124)
- paper fastener
- wipe-off pens (one per player)
- dictionary

Extension Activity

Create an eight-column chart with the following letters as headings: *E, I, J, L, N, Q, V,* and *X.* Explain that the letters on the chart are not used in the game. Then work with students to name onomatopoeic words that begin with each letter. Leave the chart on display and invite students to add words as they encounter them in everyday activities. Encourage students to refer to the chart as a reference for their own writing.

Onomatopoeia Bingo

1 Each player takes a game board and wipe-off pen. Players choose 12 different letters on the spinner to write in each box on their game board.

2 To take a turn, spin the spinner and name the letter it lands on. Check to see if that letter is on your game board.

- If so, name an onomatopoeic word that starts with that letter. Give an example of the word's use. Then look up your word on the reference key or in a dictionary. Also, ask other players if the word qualifies as a sound word. If so, write the word on the line under the letter.

- If not, your turn ends.

3 Continue taking turns. The first player to fill in four words in a row horizontally, vertically, or diagonally calls out "Onomatopoeia Bingo!" That player wins the game.

Players: 2–4

Materials

- ◎ game board
- ◎ spinner
- ◎ reference key
- ◎ wipe-off pens
- ◎ dictionary

Keep in mind that an onomatopoeic word is a word that imitates or suggests a sound.

Onomatopoeia Bingo

Write a letter from the spinner in each blank box. If you spin a letter on the game board, write a noise word that begins with that letter in the square. When you fill in four squares in a row, call out "Onomatopoeia Bingo!"

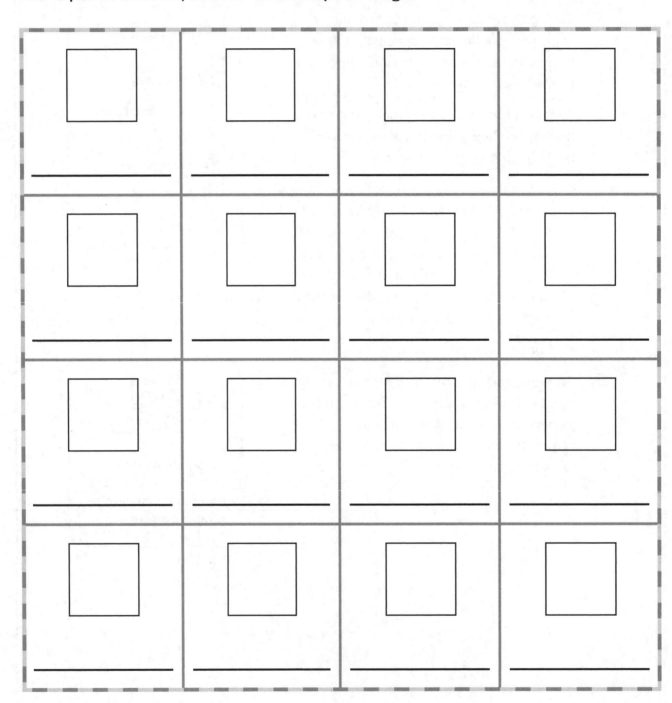

Vocabulary Games & Activities That Boost Reading and Writing Skills © 2009 by Immacula A. Rhodes. Scholastic Teaching Resources

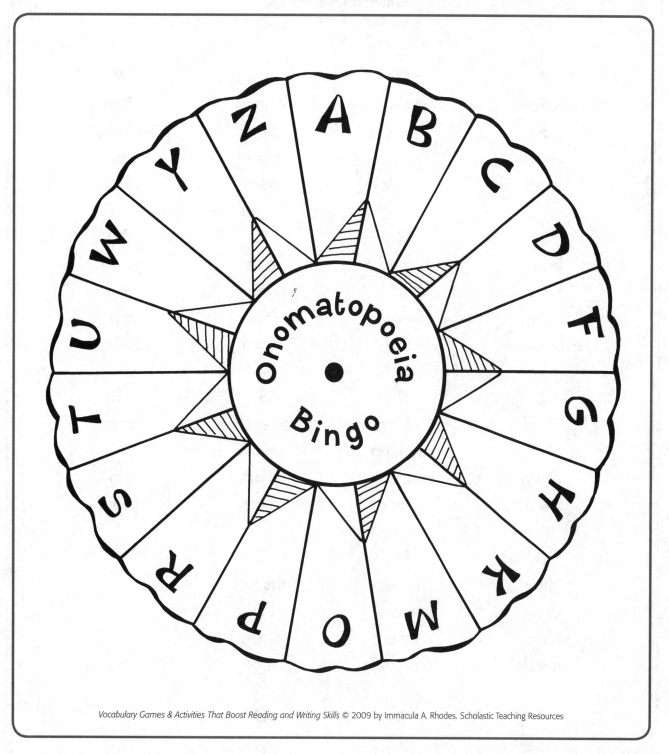

Vocabulary Games & Activities That Boost Reading and Writing Skills © 2009 by Immacula A. Rhodes. Scholastic Teaching Resources

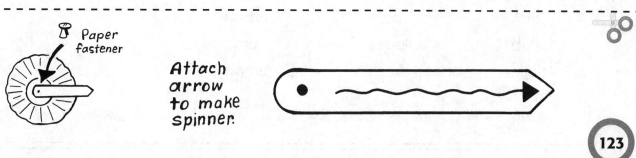

Paper fastener

Attach arrow to make spinner.

Onomatopoeia Bingo Reference Key

A
achoo
aha
ahem
argh

B
bang
beep
boing
boom

C
chirp
chug
clang
creak

D
ding
dong
drip
drizzle

F
fizz
flick
flub
flutter

G
growl
grunt
gulp
gurgle

H
hiccup
honk
hoot
howl

K
ka-blam
ka-ching
kerplunk
knock

M
meow
moan
moo
mumble

O
oink
ooh
ooze
ouch

P
patter
plop
pow
purr

R
rattle
ring
roar
rustle

S
screech
smack
snort
splash

T
thump
tick
tinkle
toot

U
ugh
uh-oh
um
umph

W
wham
whimper
whir
whoa

Y
yawn
yelp
yip
yoo-hoo

Z
zap
zing
zip
zoom

Shortcut Word Shop

Students identify clipped words and the longer versions of these words.

Players: 2–4

Skill: Identifying clipped words

Getting Ready

Copy the Directions for Play, game board, game cards, game markers, and answer key. Color the game board and markers. Laminate all game components, then cut apart the cards. Copy a supply of record sheets.

Teaching Tips

Explain what clipped words are—words that have been shortened or "clipped." Name some examples of words that have commonly used clipped versions, such as *caravan* (*van*), *examination* (*exam*), *graduate* (*grad*), and *hamburger* (*burger*). Invite students to brainstorm other words and their clipped versions. Then review the words on the game cards and challenge students to name their clipped versions.

Materials

- Directions for Play (page 126)
- Shortcut Word Shop game board, game cards, record sheet, game markers, and answer key (pages 127–131)
- coin
- pencils

Extension Activity

When some words are shortened, the spelling of their clipped versions may change so that they make sense—and in some cases, follow pronunciation rules. Show students a few examples of clipped words with altered spellings, such as *bicycle/bike, cucumber/cuke, microphone/mike, moving picture/movie, refrigerator/fridge* and *sergeant/sarge.* Then write each of these words on separate index cards, along with other clipped word pairs not used in the game. Invite students to play a game of concentration with the cards. (Other word pairs to include are: *cabriolet/cab, chrysanthemum/mum, fabulous/fab, pantaloons/pants, referee/ref,* and *rehabilitation/rehab.*)

Shortcut Word Shop

1 Shuffle the cards and stack them facedown. Each player takes a record sheet and game marker. Players place their markers on any empty space on the game board.

2 The first player tosses the coin. If it lands on "heads," move one space. If it lands on "tails, "move two spaces.

3 Follow the directions on the space. Did you land on a pair of scissors?

- If so, take a card from the top of the stack. Read the word aloud and give an example of how it is used.

- What is the clipped word that comes from that word? Say the word.

4 Check the answer key. Is your clipped word correct?

- If so, write the full word (from the card) on the long line on your record sheet. Write the clipped version next to the scissors. Then write a sentence using the full word. Underline the part of that word that is used as a clipped version.

- If not, place the card on the bottom of the stack.

5 Continue taking turns. The game ends when a player fills in all the spaces on his or her record sheet. (Or continue until all players fill in their record sheets.)

Players: 2–4

Materials

- game board
- game cards
- game markers
- record sheet
- answer key
- coin
- pencils

- Keep in mind that a clipped word is a word that has been shortened or "clipped."

- Players may invite others to share what they know about their clipped words.

- Players fill in their record sheet from top to bottom.

Shortcut Word Shop

Skip a turn.

Take another turn.

Move back 1 space.

Move ahead 1 space.

Move ahead 1 space.

Cards

Take another turn.

Shortcut Word Shop Game Cards

advertisement	crocodile	gasoline
automobile	delicatessen	gymnasium
caravan	dormitory	hamburger
cellular phone	examination	helicopter
champion	fanatic	hippopotamus
condominium	frankfurter	influenza

laboratory	miniature	teenager
limousine	popular	telephone
luncheon	preparation	tuxedo
mathematics	promenade	typographical error
mayonnaise	rhinoceros	veterinarian
memorandum	submarine	zoological garden

Name: _____

Date: _____

Shortcut Word Shop Record Sheet

Write the complete word and its clipped version on the left. Write a sentence using the complete word on the right. Underline the part of the word that is used as the clipped word.

Word		Sentence
1.	✂	
2.	✂	
3.	✂	
4.	✂	
5.	✂	
6.	✂	
7.	✂	
8.	✂	

Game Markers

Fold on gray line.

Vocabulary Games & Activities That Boost Reading and Writing Skills © 2009 by Immacula A. Rhodes. Scholastic Teaching Resources

Word	Clipped Version	Word	Clipped Version
advertisement	ad	laboratory	lab
automobile	auto	limousine	limo
caravan	van	luncheon	lunch
cellular phone	cell	mathematics	math
champion	champ	mayonnaise	mayo
condominium	condo	memorandum	memo
crocodile	croc	miniature	mini
delicatessen	deli	popular	pop
dormitory	dorm	preparation	prep
examination	exam	promenade	prom
fanatic	fan	rhinoceros	rhino
frankfurter	frank	submarine	sub
gasoline	gas	teenager	teen
gymnasium	gym	telephone	phone
hamburger	burger	tuxedo	tux
helicopter	copter	typographical error	typo
hippopotamus	hippo	veterinarian	vet
influenza	flu	zoological garden	zoo

Around the World With Words

Students explore the meanings and uses of words borrowed from other languages.

Players: 4–6

Skill: Using borrowed words

Getting Ready

Copy the Directions for Play, spinner, arrow, and word cards. Color the spinner. Laminate all game components, then cut apart the spinner, arrow, and word cards. Use the paper fastener to attach the arrow to the spinner.

Teaching Tips

- As you review the words from the game cards and word list (pages 135–137 and 144), point out that some might be used for different parts of speech or have additional meanings. For example, *doodle* is both a noun (a drawing) and a verb (*scribbling*). As a noun, *barbecue* can mean a food cooked outdoors or a grill used for cooking, while its verb form means to cook food outdoors. When playing the game, encourage students to consider whether each word has additional meanings or uses and to use a dictionary to check.

- Explain that many words students encounter are "borrowed" words—words that come from other languages. Share a few examples and tell what language they came from, such as *pretzel* and *noodle* (German), *clarinet* (French), *zero* (Italian), and *chocolate* and *barbecue* (Spanish). Use the word list (page 144) as a resource; students who speak other languages may also be a good resource.

Materials

- Directions for Play (page 133)
- Around the World With Words spinner, arrow, and word cards (pages 134–137)
- paper fastener
- write-on board
- wipe-off pen
- paper and pencils
- dictionary

Extension Activity

To help students apply their knowledge of borrowed words, place the word cards in a center along with paper and pencils. Working with partners, have students take five cards each and write a sentence using each word, leaving a blank where the word goes. (Tell students to keep the words a secret from their partners.) They can also draw pictures to go with their sentences. When finished, have students exchange sentences and cards and match the word on each card to the sentence it completes. Encourage them to use context clues and what they know about the words and their meanings. Students might also choose words from the list on page 144 for this activity.

Around the World With Words

1 Players sit in a circle around the game spinner. Shuffle the cards and stack them facedown. Have a write-on board and wipe-off pen to share.

2 To take a turn, select the top card from the stack and do the following:

- Read the word aloud. Use the pronunciation key to help you say it correctly.

- Write the word on the write-on board.

- Tell the language that the word comes from.

- Tell the meaning of the word.

3 Spin the spinner three times. Follow the directions after each spin. Do the directions tell you to call on another player?

- If so, name the player. Ask that player to use what he or she learned about the word to respond.

- If the player needs help, invite others to give clues or examples to help out.

- If you land on the same space more than once, spin again.

4 Continue taking turns. The game ends when all the cards have been used.

Players: 4–6

Materials

- ⊙ spinner
- ⊙ word cards
- ⊙ write-on board
- ⊙ wipe-off pen
- ⊙ paper and pencils
- ⊙ dictionary

- ⊙ Players may use a dictionary to look up how a word is used, or any other information they might want to know, such as additional meanings, different parts of speech, or synonyms.

- ⊙ After players respond, others may share what they know about the word.

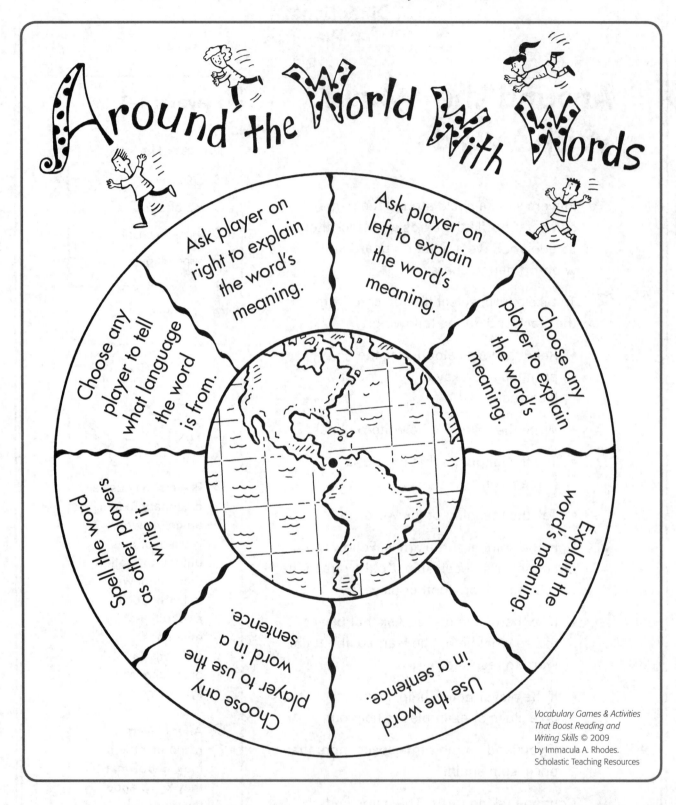

Around the World With Words

Ask player on right to explain the word's meaning.

Ask player on left to explain the word's meaning.

Choose any player to tell what language the word is from.

Choose any player to explain the word's meaning.

Spell the word as other players write it.

Explain the word's meaning.

Choose any player to use the word in a sentence.

Use the word in a sentence.

Vocabulary Games & Activities That Boost Reading and Writing Skills © 2009 by Immacula A. Rhodes. Scholastic Teaching Resources

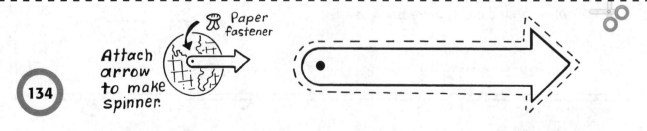

Paper fastener

Attach arrow to make spinner.

adobe (uh-**doh**-bee)

Language: Spanish

Meaning: a house made of clay

ballet (ba-**lay**)

Language: French

Meaning: a kind of dance

bangle (**bang**-guhl)

Language: Hindi

Meaning: a bracelet or anklet

bizarre (bi-zahr)

Language: French

Meaning: strange or unusual

bungalow (**buhng**-guh-loh)

Language: Hindi

Meaning: a low house with a front porch

canyon (**kan**-yuhn)

Language: Spanish

Meaning: a deep, narrow valley (often a river runs through it)

delicatessen (del-i-ka-**tes**-en)

Language: German

Meaning: a store that sells meats, cheeses, salads, and unusual foods

depot (**dee**-poh)

Language: French

Meaning: a railroad or bus station

doodle (**dood**-l)

Language: German

Meaning: to scribble

easel (**ee**-zuhl)

Language: Dutch

Meaning: a stand used to hold an artist's work

garage (guh-**rahzh**)

Language: French

Meaning: a building where a car is kept

hickory (**hik**-uh-ree)

Language: Native American

Meaning: a type of tree

iceberg (**ise**-berg)

Language: Dutch

Meaning: a large piece of floating ice

igloo (**ig**-loo)

Language: Native American

Meaning: a dome-shaped house made of blocks of snow

loot (loot)

Language: Hindi

Meaning: to steal something

kayak (**ki**-ak)

Language: Native American

Meaning: a type of canoe with a small opening in the top

kindergarten (**kin**-der-gahr-tn)

Language: German

Meaning: a class that prepares children for first grade

mustang (**muhs**-tang)

Language: Spanish

Meaning: a horse

opera (**op**-er-uh)

Language: Italian

Meaning: a musical story

origami (or-uh-**gah**-mee)

Language: Japanese

Meaning: the art of folding paper into shapes

plaza (**plah**-zuh)

Language: Spanish

Meaning: a public square or marketplace

sleigh (slay)

Language: Dutch

Meaning: a sled pulled by horses or reindeer

spaghetti (spuh-**get**-ee)

Language: Italian

Meaning: long strings of pasta

soy (soi)

Language: Japanese

Meaning: a type of bean

toboggan (tuh-**bog**-uhn)

Language: Native American

Meaning: a long, narrow sled used for coasting over snow or ice

trampoline (tram-puh-**leen**)

Language: Italian

Meaning: a springboard used for exercise or fun

tycoon (tie-**koon**)

Language: Japanese

Meaning: a rich or powerful person

veranda (vuh-**ran**-duh)

Language: Hindi

Meaning: a porch

yacht (yot)

Language: Dutch

Meaning: a sailboat used for cruising or racing

zucchini (zoo-**kee**-nee)

Language: Italian

Meaning: a long, green squash

Prefixes

Prefix	Meaning	Example
un-	not	unhappy, uncover
re-	again	replay, rewrite
in-	not	invisible, indirect
im-	not	impossible, immature
dis-	not, opposite of	dishonest, disagree
en-	to make	enable, endanger
non-	not	nonfiction, nonsense
over-	too much	overdo, oversensitive
mis-	badly	misbehave, misplace
sub-	under	subzero, subtitle
pre-	before	prepaid, preview
de-	away, from	depart, decode
trans-	across	transplant, transform
super-	over or above	supermarket, superhuman

Vocabulary Games & Activities That Boost Reading and Writing Skills © 2009 by Immacula A. Rhodes. Scholastic Teaching Resources

Suffixes

Suffix	Meaning	Example
-ing	action or process	watching, reading
-ly	in a manner of	quickly, smoothly
-er	more	stronger, neater
-est	most	greatest, meanest
-ion, -tion -ation, -ition	action or process	invention, addition, imitation
-able, -ible	can be done	profitable, sensible
-ness	condition of	hardness, awareness
-ment	action or process	government, excitement
-en	made of	wooden, golden
-ive, -ative, -itive	having the nature of	active, talkative
-ful	full of	helpful, beautiful
-less	without	motionless, useless
-al	relating to	historical, comical
-ize	to make or become	finalize, hospitalize
-ship	a quality or condition	friendship, citizenship

Latin Roots

Root	Meaning	Example
act	do	action, interact
aud	hear	audition, audience
cept, ceive, ceipt	take, hold	concept, deceive, receipt
cog	know	recognize, cognitive
dict	say, speak	dictate, prediction
duce, duct	lead, bring	produce, deduct
fract, frag	break	fracture, fragment
ject	throw	reject, interject
man	hand	manipulate, manage
mit, mis	send	emit, submission
mot, mov, mob	move	motion, moveable, mobile
ped	foot	pedal, pedestrian
port	carry	important, transportation
pos, posit	place, put	pose, position
rupt	break	erupt, interrupt
scrib	write	transcribe, scribble
sens, sent,	feel	sensitive, sensory, sentiment
spec	look, see	spectator, inspect
sta	stand	station, stable
tract	pull, drag	tractor, subtract
vert, vers	turn	convertible, controversy
vid, vis	see	evidence, vision
voc	call	vocabulary, vocation

Vocabulary Games & Activities That Boost Reading and Writing Skills © 2009 by Immacula A. Rhodes. Scholastic Teaching Resources

Greek Roots

Root	Meaning	Example
astro	star	astrology, astronomer
auto	self	automatic, autograph
biblio	book	bibliography, bibliophile
bio	life	biology, biography
chron	time	chronicle, synchronize
cycle, cyclo	wheel, circular	bicycle, cyclone
dem	people	democrat, democracy
erg	work	energy, energetic
gen	birth, race	generation, genetic
geo	earth	geology, geography
gram	written, drawn	program, grammar
graph	written, drawn	paragraph, graphic
gno, kno	know	diagnose, knowledge
hydr, hydra, hydro	water	dehydrate, hydrant
log	idea, word, study	logical, monologue
meter	measure	centimeter, geometry
naut	ship	nautical, astronaut
nym, onym, onom	name	synonym, anonymous
path	feeling, suffering	sympathy, pathetic
phon	sound, voice	phonics, telephone
photo	light	photograph, photosynthesis
scope	to see	stethoscope, microscope
therm	heat	thermostat, hypothermia

Vocabulary Games & Activities That Boost Reading and Writing Skills © 2009 by Immacula A. Rhodes. Scholastic Teaching Resources

Heteronyms

Heteronyms are words that are spelled the same, but are pronounced differently and have different meanings.

bass: a fish; the lowest singing voice

bow: a weapon that shoots arrows; to bend the head and upper body forward

conduct: the way someone behaves; to lead a band

content: the thing that is inside something; to be happy

contest: a competition; to argue against something

contract: an agreement; to become or make something smaller

convict: a prisoner or criminal; to find someone guilty of a crime

desert: to abandon; a dry, sandy, waterless area of land

does: more than one female deer; to perform or do

dove: a bird; to have jumped headfirst into water

drawer: someone who draws; a compartment that slides in and out of a piece of furniture

graduate: a person who has received a diploma; to complete school

lead: to guide or show the way; a soft metal

live: to have life; not dead

minute: a measure of time; small

object: a thing that can be seen and touched; to disagree with something or someone

perfect: without flaws or defects; to make something flawless

permit: to allow; a paper that gives someone permission to do something

present: a gift; to give or offer something to someone

produce: to make or create; vegetables

project: an assignment; to make an estimate or guess about something

rebel: a person who resists authority or rule; to resist or oppose something

record: to write down; the best performance that has been measured and noted

refuse: unwillingness to do something; trash

relay: a race; to pass on something

separate: to divide or move apart; standing alone or disconnected

sewer: one who sews; an underground channel that carries off wastewater

subject: a topic, issue, or theme; to cause or force something onto someone else

suspect: a person thought to be guilty of a crime; to doubt the truth of something

sow: to plant seeds; a female pig

tear: to rip or pull apart; salty liquid that flows from eyes

wind: moving air; to turn in circles or wrap around something

wound: an injury; to have been turned in circles or wrapped around something

Vocabulary Games & Activities That Boost Reading and Writing Skills © 2009 by Immacula A. Rhodes. Scholastic Teaching Resources

Homophone Pairs

**Homophones are words that sound the same,
but have different spellings and meanings.**

aisle, isle	loan, lone
bald, bawled	meat, meet
band, banned	morning, mourning
blew, blue	none, nun
buy, bye	paced, paste
board, bored	pain, pane
bough, bow	peace, piece
boy, buoy	poor, pour
bread, bred	pray, prey
ceiling, sealing	rain, reign
cent, scent	rap, wrap
cheap, cheep	read, reed
chews, choose	right, write
days, daze	sail, sale
desert, dessert	shoe, shoo
fair, fare	soar, sore
flew, flu	threw, through
forth, fourth	throne, thrown
foul, fowl	tied, tide
heal, heel	toad, towed
heard, herd	wade, weighed
hole, whole	wait, weight
knows, nose	which, witch
lessen, lesson	

Vocabulary Games & Activities That Boost Reading and Writing Skills © 2009 by Immacula A. Rhodes. Scholastic Teaching Resources

Words Borrowed
From Other Languages

Dutch

bamboo
boss
caboose
cookie
cruise
drum
easel
iceberg
landscape
sleigh
waffle
yacht

French

ballet
bizarre
bureau
cabinet
café
cantaloupe
chef
clarinet
denim
depot
gallop
garage
menu
police
restaurant
shock
zero

German

delicatessen
doodle
frankfurter
hamburger
kindergarten
noodle
poodle
pretzel
waltz

Hindi

bangle
bungalow
dinghy
jungle
loot
pajamas
punch
shampoo
thug
veranda
yoga

Italian

confetti
macaroni
opera
piano
pizza
solo
studio
trampoline
umbrella
violin
volcano
zucchini

Japanese

futon
judo
origami
soy
sushi
tycoon

Native American

bayou
caucus
chipmunk
hickory
igloo
kayak
moccasin
moose

muskrat
pecan
raccoon
skunk
squash
toboggan
tomahawk

Spanish

adobe
alligator
barbecue
canoe
canyon
chili
guitar
hurricane
maize

mustang
patio
plaza
potato
ranch
rodeo
taco
tornado
tortilla